T0088472

1215
AND ALL THAT

1215
AND ALL THAT
MAGNA CARTA AND KING JOHN

ED WEST

Skyhorse Publishing

Skyhorse Publishing books may be purchased in bulk at special discounts for sales promotion, corporate gifts, fund-raising, or educational purposes. Special editions can also be created to specifications. For details, contact the Special Sales Department, Skyhorse Publishing, 307 West 36th Street, 11th Floor, New York, NY 10018 or info@skyhorsepublishing.com.

Skyhorse® and Skyhorse Publishing® are registered trademarks of Skyhorse Publishing, Inc.®, a Delaware corporation.

Visit our website at www.skyhorsepublishing.com.

10 9 8 7 6 5 4 3 2 1

Library of Congress Cataloging-in-Publication Data is available on file.

Cover design by Rain Saukas

Print ISBN: 978-1-5107- 1987-3
Ebook ISBN: 978-1-5107- 1992-7

Printed in the United States of America

Contents

No free man shall be seized, imprisoned, dispossessed, outlawed, exiled or ruined in any way, except for the lawful judgement of his peers and the laws of the land.

—Magna Carta, Clause 39

Introduction

One day in June 1944, King George VI was driving back to Windsor from London in a furious mood. The powerful wartime Prime Minister Winston Churchill had just overruled him once again, frustrating the stammering king's attempt to have a say in government. The monarch, a gentle and nervous figure who was well on his way to smoking himself to death through sheer anxiety caused by a job he didn't want and which his useless brother Edward had forced on him, happened to pass by a spot near the Thames. As his secretary Alan Lascelles later recalled: 'Suddenly he threw his arm out of the window and exclaimed "And that's where it all started!"'[1]

The place was Runnymede and it was there that, in 1215, George's ancestor King John (also the ancestor of Churchill and the US president Franklin Roosevelt)[2] was forced into a peace treaty with his leading barons that would have a profound impact on the country and the world. It came about over frustration at the misrule of the king's family, known to us as the Plantagenets, but it established fundamental principles about the rule of law that would spread to the English colonies and worldwide. This Magna Carta, as it became known later that century, would form the basis of the rule of law and due process in England and around the globe.

At the time of King George's outburst the descendants of those barons, ruling states on both sides of the Atlantic, were on the cusp of winning a worldwide existential war being fought between those who believed in the rule of law and those who didn't. Their victory would globally implement the freedoms that we have come to think of as Anglo-Saxon, although in the context of this story we might better call them Anglo-Norman, created as they were by the French-speaking aristocracy of thirteenth-century England.*

England does not really go in for national monuments, and when it does they are often eccentric. There is no great shrine to Alfred the Great, for example, who united and saved the country at the start of its history, but we do have, right in the middle of London, a large marble memorial to the animals that gave their lives in the fight against Fascism. And Runnymede, which you could say is the birthplace of English liberty, would be a deserted wood were it not for the Americans. Beside the Thames, some ten miles outside London's western suburbs, this place 'between Windsor and Staines,' as it is called in the original document, is a rather subdued spot, with the sound of constant traffic close by and in the distance that of the M25 motorway and airplanes landing and taking off at Heathrow Airport. Crossing the A308 from the other side of the road is actually quite hazardous, and once there you'd have no idea it was a momentous place if it wasn't for an enclosure with a small Romanesque circus, paid for by the American Association of Lawyers in 1957.

American lawyers are possibly not the most well-loved group on earth, but it would be an awful world without them, and for that we must thank the men who on June 15, 1215, forced the king of England to agree to a document, 'The Great Charter of the Liberties.'

---

*   Of the twenty-five rebels who brought about Magna Carta, sixteen had a surname beginning with 'de.'

Magna Carta was not the first time a king had made such a contract. Two centuries earlier in 1014, the hopeless Ethelred II gave a similar promise after returning to the kingdom from which the Danes had kicked him out; he was so unpopular that his subjects were fairly ambivalent about whether they wanted Ethelred back after the death of the Viking pirate-king Sweyn Forkbeard who had seized the throne. Since then, various monarchs had made promises about ruling with the consent of the people, which they usually ignored.

Long before Ethelred's time, the Anglo-Saxons held witans and had some vague idea of the law being something that belonged to everyone, although how much of this is myth making from the seventeenth century is a matter of debate. Runnymede may have been the site of a witan in the past—*ruineg* perhaps being a regular meeting—but we cannot know for sure, and what happened in 1215 was most definitely fundamentally different. It established not just restraints on the monarch but also the rule of law, no arrest without charge, just cause and other essential principles.

Although John went back on the agreement almost immediately, and the country fell into civil war, by the end of the century Magna Carta had been written into English law; today, eight hundred years later, it is considered the most important legal document in history. As the great eighteenth-century statesman William Pitt the Elder put it, Magna Carta is 'the Bible of the English Constitution.'

Two weeks before the king's dressing down by Churchill, the armies of the democracies had landed in Normandy, the ancestral home of the kings of England, and from where they had made the reverse journey nine centuries earlier. The victories by English-speaking forces the following year would not just crush Nazism but make the ideas of 1215 universal, worldwide values, even if in much of the world they remain unenforceable and theoretical.

How did this all happen here in England? The story begins a hundred years earlier with some drunken sailors in the English Channel.

CHAPTER ONE

Henry I's Charter

King Henry never smiled again after being told of his son's death. Seventeen-year-old William had joined two hundred revelers on a famed vessel called the *White Ship* sailing from Normandy to England late at night on November 25, 1120. The atmosphere was boisterous, and when priests arrived to bless the boat they were waved away with drunken jeers and laughter. On board were the cream of the Anglo-Norman ruling class, whose grandfathers had won England under William the Conqueror, including two of the king's illegitimate children. Henry's nephew, Stephen of Blois, was due to sail but could not drink because of a stomach condition and was so unnerved by the hugely drunk state of the crew that he left and got back ashore. When the ship hit rocks, barely out of Barfleur harbor, William dragged himself to a lifeboat but went back for his half sister Matilda, one of the king's many bastards. They both drowned, along with everyone on board, except for one, a baker who had gone on board to get some money and who was sober.

The national tragedy would bring about a civil war called the 'Shipwreck' or 'Anarchy' in which Henry's only surviving legitimate child Matilda (not to be confused with the Matilda who drowned on the ship) fought for control of the kingdom with her cousin Stephen, who had claimed the throne on his uncle's death in 1135 (despite going out of his way to pledge his loyalty to Matilda when Henry was alive). It would end in the rise of a new dynasty, the Plantagenets, whose relentless greed provoked the leading barons into bringing about Magna Carta.

Henry I had come to power after his elder brother William II, called 'Rufus' because of his alcohol-soaked red face, had died in a mysterious hunting accident in 1100. Their father William the Conqueror had won the kingdom at the Battle of Hastings on October 14, 1066, and his twenty-one-year reign was one of almost unparalleled repression and violence, the most brutal episode being the harrying of the north in 1069 in which as many as two hundred thousand people died in Yorkshire.* It's fair to say that after this he wasn't tremendously popular, but by the period's definitions of success he had been a great king, while his son had been a dreary failure.

Rufus had spent his reign in conflict with both the Church and with his elder brother Robert, who had succeeded as Duke of Normandy despite the mutual loathing he and his father had for each other. This brotherly feud was suspended in 1095 when Pope Urban II called for a Crusade to win back the Holy Land for Christendom, and Robert volunteered, mortgaging Normandy to pay for it. Robert was on his way back with a new, very rich wife in 1100 when Rufus was fatally wounded by an arrow in the New Forest, with his brother Henry conveniently close enough to reach the Treasury at Winchester within an hour to claim the crown.† Six years later, he invaded Normandy where he captured his surviving brother and kept him imprisoned for the rest of his life; by the time Robert died, in 1134, he had been in jail for so long he even had time to learn Welsh.

---

*   See *1066 and Before All That*, the second book in the series.
†   Hunting was a dangerous sport and accidents were quite frequent–the Conqueror's second son Richard had also been killed around 1081 in the very same forest–but the circumstances of the king's death was extremely fortunate for Henry.

The new king needed to win over three groups upon his accession. Firstly, the Church; secondly, the barons, the vastly powerful one hundred or so Norman landowners who had come over with William the Conqueror; and finally the English themselves, who constituted around 98 percent of the population.

To help justify his rule, Henry issued a Charter of Liberties in 1100, promising to honor the laws of Edward the Confessor, the last king from the old House of Wessex, whose death in 1066 had sparked the Norman invasion. By the sounds of it, Henry had no intention whatsoever of keeping any of his promises, and neither did any of his successors, but that wasn't the point. New kings as far back as ancient Babylon have pledged to rule within the laws and customs of the people, so this wasn't that unusual, but Henry I's coronation charter was important because it influenced the barons of 1215, something we know because a sort of early draft of Magna Carta turned up in the nineteenth century referring to it.

This being an age when much of the population were toothless simpletons and not well versed in politics, most of the twenty clauses of 1100 only involved the rights of barons and the Church, in particular the lives of widows and heirs. Henry's charter was very much a product of what is now called the feudal system, a phrase that was only coined in 1776 by Adam Smith but which fairly accurately describes the era. After winning power William the Conqueror had drastically changed the social hierarchy, dispossessing the upper layer of English society, the five thousand *thegns* (literally 'one who serves'), and replacing them with a small number of barons. As the overlord to these barons, the king had certain rights, including power over widows and orphans, and the right to take a slice of inheritance. This was considered a king's privilege but bad monarchs inevitably took advantage to fleece heirs and sell off widows. The lords in turn had the same rights over the peasants below them, the majority of whom would have been unfree serfs. The Normans didn't introduce this system, but they did increase the sharp divide between rich and poor.

In a feudal system, all lords derived their land from the monarch, and so were obliged to pay a fee to pass their title to their son; there were also sometimes disputes about who was actually the heir, and this might be costly for the king to arbitrate. So Henry's charter stated that 'If any baron or earl of mine shall die, his heirs shall not be forced to purchase their inheritance, but shall retrieve it through force of law and custom.' Henry promised that he would only charge a 'legitimate and just relief' on barons inheriting their father's lands, whatever 'just' meant. He pledged that wives would also be allowed to inherit their husband's land, and would not be forced by the king to take another husband, so that 'Any widow who wishes to remarry should consult with me, but I shall abide by the wishes of her close relatives, the other barons and earls.' As long as her new husband was not 'one of my enemies.'

The rights of man it was not; and in the words of one historian: 'During his thirty-five-year reign, Henry I kept virtually none of the promises set out in his coronation charter.'[1]

By condemning the 'oppressive practices which have been an evil presence in England,' Henry was also shoring up his own legitimacy and making himself look better, the trick of all politicians down the ages of exaggerating the faults of the previous regime. But it did to some extent reaffirm the idea of one law for all, an essential aspect of the 1215 document. Clause 8 of Henry's charter stated that 'If any of my barons commit a crime, he shall not bind himself to the crown with a payment as was done in the time of my father and brother, but shall stand for the crime as was custom and law before the time of my father, and make amends as are appropriate.'

Henry ruled for thirty-five years, and his harsh enforcement of laws, at a time when the country was absurdly dangerous by modern standards, was generally popular: executing a few people always went down quite well. On one occasion in Leicester in 1124 'they hanged. . . . more thieves than had ever been hanged before . . . in all forty-four men in that little time; and six men were blinded and castrated.'[2] The people loved him.

He also shored up his power by marrying Matilda, who was the daughter of the King of Scotland but more importantly a great-granddaughter of the Anglo-Saxon king Edmund Ironside, which cemented the legitimacy of an otherwise foreign dynasty. Her real name was Edith, but that was too complicated for the Normans, so Henry just gave her the same name as his mother.

However, after the *White Ship* disaster the country faced a succession crisis: Henry had a daughter, another Matilda (young William also had a widow called Matilda while Stephen's wife was called Matilda too—they weren't very imaginative with names at the time) but she was, obviously, a woman and although Henry forced the nobles to swear an oath to her, when he died in 1135 (by the curious cause of overdosing on lampreys, a type of eel) his nephew Stephen seized the throne and most of the barons supported him. Like his uncle, he proclaimed a coronation charter, declaring that he would rule according to custom and law, but he never had much time to do anything about it. There followed a civil war between supporters of the two cousins, a conflict described as 'nineteen long winters when Christ and his saints slept' by the *Anglo-Saxon Chronicle*, the clerical records established by Alfred the Great in the ninth century that gave a sort of news account of the usually dreadful events that befell the kingdom.

Matilda almost won by capturing London in 1141 but proved so unpopular that she was forced to flee to Oxford. The following year she escaped from yet another angry mob in that city dressed entirely in white during a snowstorm. By some accounts, and obviously a lot of them were biased, Matilda had a knack for rubbing people the wrong way; she had been sent to Germany at the age of eight to marry the Holy Roman Emperor Heinrich V, who was twenty-nine, which is a little weird, and from eleven had effectively ruled the empire while he was out on endless wars, until he died at the age of thirty-eight (of cancer, of all things, not a classic disease for a medieval warrior king, although maybe it was a stressful job).

A widow in her twenties, she was now betrothed to the fifteen-year-old Geoffrey of Anjou, from a line of aristocrats famously cruel, even by the standards of the period. The Normans hugely disliked the Angevins, seeing them as needlessly violent, which, coming from the Normans, is saying something, but the marriage was necessary for geographic reasons. A week before the wedding, Henry I had knighted Geoffrey in Rouen, the Norman capital, the adolescent dressed in purple, wearing double-mail armor with gold spurs, and a sword supposedly forged by the Norse god Wayland the Smith. Geoffrey also wore a shrub called a *planta genista* on his lapel that he used as a sort of camouflage while out hunting, and so his dynasty came to be known as the Plantagenets (although not until the 1450s, when the last remnants of the family were busily engaged in killing each other).

The Anarchy came to an end after Stephen's awful-sounding son Eustace choked to death in 1153 while sacking an abbey, and the king agreed to pass the throne to Geoffrey and Matilda's teen-aged son Henry Fitzempress after his death; this came to pass the following year.

CHAPTER TWO

The Family from Hell

Henry II was to become a great king who would revolutionize the English state, in particular creating the jury system, but he and his family were also notoriously cruel, greedy, and violent. So when Magna Carta emerged it was not only aimed at John, but at the whole Plantagenet dynasty who had come to power in 1154. John was just the most incompetent of them, while his son Henry III, whose reign saw a second barons' uprising that led to the creation of a 'Parliament,' was a simpleton.

This cruelty seemed to run deep: the dynasty's founder, Geoffrey of Anjou's great-great-grandfather Fulk the Black, was a cheery-sounding fellow with unusual interests in sexual degradations. Although notoriously violating anything that moved, he could be a bit jealous, and had his first wife burned at the stake in her wedding dress in the middle of the marketplace in Angers on discovering her adultery with a goatherd. He then burned down the town a few years later. When Fulk put down a rebellion by Geoffrey the Hammer, his equally awful son, 'he made him crawl around the floor in front of his courtiers, saddled and bridled like a horse, begging for mercy, while his father screamed, "you're broken in, broken in!"'[1] Later on a trip to the Holy Land, Fulk made his servants flog him through the streets of Jerusalem as he howled for forgiveness. It's possible all wasn't entirely well with him, mentally.

Geoffrey Plantaganet's grandfather, Fulk the Quarreler, had imprisoned his own brother and divorced three of his five wives, while he was described by chronicler Orderic Vitalis as 'a man with many reprehensible, even scandalous, habits,' whatever that means. Geoffrey was not exactly a progressive, either; having ruled Normandy from 1144, while his wife was fighting Stephen in England, he had gained a reputation for extreme cruelty. When the canons of Sees elected as bishop one Arnulf, a man whom Geoffrey didn't like, he had him castrated, and the churchmen had to walk through the city holding the poor man's penis in a basin to show that he was not qualified as bishop.

The popular story of the Angevin family origins was that while out hunting, Fulk the Black's grandfather had met and married a lady called Melusine, who was very mysterious and very beautiful and who gave him four sons. However, he began to grow suspicious when at church she always left before Holy Communion, and eventually the husband ordered his knights to grab her as she exited—but she slipped out of her cloak and flew off with two sons under her arms, leaving the other two. This was Gerald of Wales's story, at any rate, although he did admittedly hate the royal family. Another chronicler, Walter Map, said that Melusine was a sort of dragon, who shrieked horribly as she disappeared through the roof of the church. Map also said the Plantagenets were heirs to the mythological huntsman, King Herlequin, the leader of a group of devils who would haunt the northern coast of France (this French myth evolved into harlequins, who aren't devils as such but are still slightly sinister figures).

The less interesting truth is that the Plantagenets probably originated with a Breton outlaw called Tertulle the Forester, a sort of bandit in the ninth century who fought the Vikings in the Loire Valley and came to rule his own mini-kingdom in western France.

But later subjects of the Plantagenets would claim that Satan himself was the ultimate dynastic founder, which suggests that the royal family's PR team faced something of an uphill struggle at the time. Henry II's son Richard the Lionheart joked that 'We come from the Devil and we'll end by going to the Devil.' Typical of the popular view of the family was that of a mystic called Godric of Finchale, who once had a vision in which King Henry II and his four sons prostrated themselves in a church and climbed up to the altar where they began to clean the crucifix. But as they reached the top of the cross 'horrible to relate, they began to defile the altar on every side with their urine and excrement.'[2]

Henry II came to the throne at an exciting time; as the twelfth century was a period of tremendous economic and cultural growth in Europe, an explosion in some ways as dramatic as the Renaissance three centuries later. It saw the building of the great Gothic cathedrals, the growth of the first universities, the philosophy of Thomas Aquinas and Albert the Great, new and exciting ways of killing people in war, and a rapidly expanding economy and population. There was a huge rediscovery of Greek thinking, much of it through contact with the Muslim world; two Englishmen, Adelard of Bath and Robert of Chester, helped base western science on *Elements* of Euclid and Ptomley's *Almagest* through Latin translations of Arabic copies of the original Greek; Adelard also helped to introduce Arabic numerals to Europe.

There was also a great breakthrough in technology, with inventions such as paper (first recorded around 1100), clocks, oil painting, compasses, buttons for clothes, and mirrors. The center of this burgeoning renaissance was Paris and its university, where between 1179 and 1215 one-third of all students were English.

Europe was also becoming less barbaric. The Normans ate in big halls where food was thrown onto the floor, where it was quickly grabbed by dogs and beggars who were allowed to hang around for scraps, but in the twelfth century came the *Liber Urbani*, the *Book of the Civilized Man.* This advised people 'when, where and how to belch, defecate, fart, spit and urinate politely' and stated among other things that 'only the head of household, for example, was entitled to urinate in the hall.' It was the beginning of etiquette or 'courtesy,' although the fact that guests had to be instructed not to pee in the hallway suggests they had some ways, to go.[3]

But in England, in particular, the twelfth century also saw the emergence of a centralized state and legal system, with law courts, proper records, and juries. In charge of it was the rapacious monarchy, growing in size and hungry for money, and resented by the people funding it; an indication of the Crown's growth can be seen in its ownership of castles, so that while in 1154, the monarch held 35 percent of England's 350 fortresses, by John's reign it owned nearly half of them.

Geoffrey's son, who took power in 1154, was described by Gerald of Wales as 'a man of reddish, freckled complexion, with a large, round head, grey eyes that glowed fiercely then grew bloodshot in anger, a fierce countenance and a harsh, cracked voice.' From an early age, Henry II had shown the sort of spirit that made great medieval kings: as a thirteen-year-old he'd had taken a group of heavily armed friends over to England and demanded money from King Stephen. The monarch agreed to his charming young cousin's menaces, and six years later handed over the entire kingdom.

By the time Henry became King of England and Duke of Normandy, he was already ruler of his native Anjou, and by the age of twenty-two he controlled the entire west coast of France. He also went on to invade Ireland, a decision that down the years has caused one or two problems.[4]

This first Angevin king was highly intelligent, and as well as being able to read and write (he was one of only a few kings in medieval times known to read in bed), Henry could speak at least passable English, Latin, two types of French, and Welsh. He had a good memory and knowledge of history, and could converse with people of education, although his tastes weren't that highbrow. His favorite court jester was one Roland the Farter, who was given a manor in Suffolk on condition that every Christmas he 'gave a jump, a whistle and a fart before Henry and his courtiers.' It was not a time of great courtly sophistication, although in fairness Roland apparently trained himself to fart whole tunes.

Full of nervous energy and very fidgety, the king was described as a 'human chariot dragging all after him' and was always on his feet, which was a pain as courtiers were not allowed to sit while he stood. He was unable to stay still, even at Mass, and would travel around his realm, drafting laws and hearing cases, his underlings having to sleep in woodlands and fighting over who got the pigsty while the king lay in a nice comfy bed.

Intelligent and energetic, the king could also be stubborn, and once he decided he didn't like someone, he never changed his opinion of them. However, Henry's main problem was his temper, and as a result he spent his entire reign fighting. Once, believing that a servant had betrayed him, he 'aflame into his usual rage, flung his cap from his head, pulled off his belt, threw off his cloak and clothes, grabbed the silken coverlet off the couch, and sitting as it might be on some dung heap started chewing pieces of straw as if he were sitting in a ditch.' The servant in question had said something positive about the king of the Scots, which Henry took as a slight. On another occasion, the king accused his butler, Robert Belet, of insolence because he had not given him a sparrowhawk as a present; Belet was forced to pay a fine of £100, which according to records he was still shelling out eighteen years later. Another of his men, Henry of Essex, dropped the king's banner during an invasion of Wales in 1157, and was forced to undergo trial by ordeal. His opponent beat him and his lands were confiscated, with Henry of Essex left for dead; however, he recovered and lived for another thirteen miserable years as a monk.

The king's furious temper would aggravate the central conflict of the era—with the Church, St. Thomas Becket's murder being one of the few medieval events that has stuck in the public consciousness; but it also fueled the far more hateful war with his own sons, four of the most monstrous individuals of the period.

William of Newburgh said Henry 'was hateful to nearly everyone,' and he certainly had a vicious streak. During his standoff with the Church, hundreds of Thomas Becket's supporters were stripped of possessions, exiled, or imprisoned in chains; clerics could even have their eyes gouged out or genitals hacked off, while a young man who took the king a message from the Pope was blinded and forced to drink boiling water.[5] There was also a notorious incident in 1165 when Henry had taken young people hostage in Wales and ordered all the males to be blinded and castrated while the females had their noses and ears cut off.

But, to be fair, Henry was one of the less cruel members of his family.

Eleanor

As well as his land in England, Normandy, and Anjou, Henry had acquired another huge chunk of territory two years before he became king by marrying the slightly risqué Eleanor of Aquitaine. Eleanor was a divorcée previously wed to King Louis VII of France and was so scandalous that a gossipy English monk, called Richard of Devizes, observed none-too-subtly that: 'Many know what I would that none of us knew. Let no one say any more about it. I know too well. Keep silent.' Henry's father Geoffrey had also supposedly 'personally verified Eleanor's appetite for passion before recommending her to his son,'[6] which says something about how messed up the family was.

Eleanor was one of the most culturally influential people of the medieval period, both in France and England, to a large part helping to create our idea of romance. She came from the intensely passionate and sensual region of Aquitaine, now southwest France but at that time an entirely separate country with its own language, culture, and mind-set.

Eleanor's grandfather Duke Guilhelm (William) IX was a 'crusader, womanizer and poet of love and loss—the first of the troubedours,' that is the romantic poets of Aquitaine.[7] William of Malmesbury had 'recounted scandalous rumors of the duke's provocative exploits and his sardonic wit,' among which that 'he ordered that his mistress's portrait should be painted on his shield . . . declaring that "it was his will to bear her in battle as she had borne him in bed."' The Aquitainians matched corny romance with deep faith, and Eleanor's father Guilhelm X had died on pilgrimage to the relics of St. James at Compostenla in Spain. Eleanor, therefore, became duchess aged only twelve or at most fifteen, an incredibly eligible heiress who brought with her one of the fertile regions of Europe, including the best wine producing area in the world. Had she looked like Shrek she would have been a great catch, but as it was she was also fiercely intelligent and beautiful.*

Eleanor was the epitome of sultry Latin sensuality, while her husband Louis was the height of northern European uptightness. The royal couple were comically mismatched.

At the time the King of France, Louis the Fat, was dying of dysentery but was keen to have Aquitaine to add to his realm. He had arranged for Eleanor to marry his eldest son Philip, but unfortunately he was killed after tripping up on a stray pig in Paris (just one of those twelfth-century hazards). Instead, she was wed to Philip's younger brother Louis, who had been educated to be a cleric by Suger, the abbot of St. Denis near Paris and one of the greatest minds of the age. It wasn't ideal, for 'Louis was too pious and rigid

---

*   A German song from the period went:

   Were the world all mine
   From the sea to the Rhine
   I'd give it all
   If so be the Queen of England
   Lay in my arms.

for his young, beautiful, and vivacious wife, who declared that she had married a monk not a king.'[8] The younger Louis was 'by all accounts, besotted with his wife, offering her an infatuated, puppyish devotion,'[9] but it was never going to be enough, even when he massacred over a thousand people in order to prove himself to her.

The notorious incident happened after the king had arranged for Eleanor's sister Petronilla to marry his cousin Raoul. Raoul, however, was already married and Petronilla was engaged to a count, Theobald of Blois and Champagne, and so naturally the Pope didn't approve. Nor did Theobald, obviously, and in an effort to show his masculine dominance to his wife, Louis marched into Champagne and at Viray killed 1,300 people who had hidden in a church, burning it down.

The newlyweds soon got to see the world when Louis took his young wife on crusade, which turned out to be a bit of a disaster. While the Arabs had conquered Jerusalem almost four centuries earlier, it was the arrival of the Seljuk Turks, a threat to the eastern Christians of Constantinople, which had inspired the western Catholic Church to try to conquer back the Near East. Although the crusade had been preached by Pope Urban II, much of the original drive had come from an obscure figure called Peter the Hermit, who led a huge army of peasants and desperados across Europe before most were slaughtered in the Middle East, if not before. The crusaders had conquered Jerusalem in 1099, and this led to the establishment of a number of Christian kingdoms on the coast of what is now Lebanon and Israel, in a region they called 'Outremere' ('overseas'). However, while the original crusaders had settled down and even began to trade with their Muslim neighbors, they were soon disrupted by new arrivals eager to fight a holy war in a region they knew absolutely nothing about, 'newcomers from the west who were both stupidly aggressive and aggressively stupid,' in the words of one historian.'[10] The result was endless conflict.

The trigger for the new crusade was a series of disasters that befell the crusader kingdoms. Bohemund II, prince of Antioch, was fighting some Christian Armenians when the Turks came along and cut his head off, the local emir having it embalmed and sent to the Caliph of Baghdad, who was said to be delighted. Then in 1131, Baldwin II of Jerusalem had died while fighting, leaving a daughter, and Geoffrey of Anjou's father Fulk came all the way from Flanders to marry this Melisende on the understanding that he would become king. However, the crusaders soon fell out among themselves after rumors Melisende was having an affair with the Lord of Jaffa, and then Fulk died after being thrown from a horse while chasing a hare. Then the city of Edessa fell to the Muslims; this triggered a new crusade, preached by St. Bernard of Clairvaux, and among those who volunteered to take the Cross was King Louis of France.

It didn't go well; for a start Eleanor's baggage train was said to be so large it 'impaired the army's mobility'[11] and when they got to the Middle East she seems to have had an affair with her own uncle, the handsome Ramon. To start with, Ramon and Louis had disagreed over military tactics, and Eleanor took her uncle's side. 'The long, laughing conversations between uncle and niece became embarrassing for everyone,'[12] especially as the two spoke in Occitan, the language of Aquitaine, which the people of Paris couldn't understand. When Louis declared his plans to leave Antioch for Jerusalem, she refused to go with him. He remonstrated with her and she reminded him that they were actually related, implying that under Church law she could get the marriage annulled.

The royal matrimonial troubles became common knowledge and Abbot Suger wrote to Louis in 1149 saying 'we venture to congratulate you, if we may, upon the extent to which you suppress your anger.' Which must have calmed him down.

Eventually, the royal couple arrived home, after months traveling through Europe during which they were both sick most of the time. The Second Crusade achieved very little and only ended when the Muslim leader was murdered by his own dwarf. Poor uncle Ramon was killed soon after by the Arabs and his head was sent in a silver box as a trophy for the caliph of Baghdad, who must have been amassing quite a collection of heads by now.

Louis and Eleanor soon split, the pretext being how closely related they were, which the Church was very strict about at the time; soon an august assembly of French bishops at Paris ruled the marriage illegal. Although the couple had two daughters, this wasn't an issue as under French law not only could they not become monarchs but the crown could only pass through the male line.*

The marriage was over. However, Eleanor was such a catch that on her way from Paris to her homeland she was ambushed by two separate suitors hoping to win her hand by rather unorthodox means.

One of her admirers was Theobald V, the new count of Champagne, whose father had previously been attacked by Louis; she managed to avoid him, and Theobald later married Eleanor and Louis's daughter Alix.† The other was Geoffrey of Anjou, younger son of Geoffrey and Matilda, who also failed. So it was a huge shock when she was betrothed to Geoffrey's older brother Henry, with whom her husband had previously been at war, especially as Eleanor was eleven years older than her new man.

Eleanor had a lasting cultural influence in France and England, introducing the romantic poetic tradition that may have originated in her native Aquitaine, and which did much to shape medieval and so modern ideas about love. Although romantic love is presumably as old as humanity, the tradition of erotic poetry and love songs

---

* This was called the Salic Law, and would be the subject of great contention in years to come when the English king Edward III claimed the French crown through his mother.

† Theobald would later win a claim to fame by orchestrating the first blood libel in Europe against Jews. He eventually joined the Third Crusade, dying at Acre and presumably going straight to heaven.

originated in southwest France, although it may have been influenced by Persia, via Moorish Spain (there are different theories). Courtly love poems often featured repressed and impossible love between aristocratic women and knights of a lower social status whose job it was to guard them, still essentially quite a popular genre in fiction although more recently involving bodyguards or gardeners. Walter Map tells of a story of a queen who lusted after a knight called Galo, and after he got one of his friends to tell her he was a eunuch, she sent one of her ladies in waiting to seduce him and 'put her finger on the spot [and] bring back word of whether he was man or no.'

Louis was still devoted to her, but lost Eleanor and the whole of Aquitaine in possibly the worst settlement in history before the arrival of the modern divorce lawyer. Had they produced sons he would have kept her, and to add insult to costly injury she went on to produce five boys by her new, younger husband, four of them surviving to adulthood, as well as three daughters. Henry also had as many as twelve children by his various mistresses, an attraction that must have had less to do with his bloodshot eyes and enormous beer belly, and probably more to do with his massive empire stretching from the borders of Scotland to the northern tip of Spain. Notorious for his sexual appetite, Henry's court had so many prostitutes attached to it that there was a 'marshal of the whores' to deal with them, whose name was, implausibly to fans of British comedy, Baldrick.

Although under the feudal system he was technically a vassal of the King of France in his French territories, Henry was in some ways more powerful, and he and King Louis VII were great rivals, as their sons would later be. When in 1158 Henry traveled to meet his opposite number to arrange the marriage of his infant son and Louis's daughter by his second wife, he used it as an excuse to show off his country's growing wealth and status.

Among the entourage that made its way from the coast of Normandy to Paris were 250 men singing English songs, a selection of

English mastiffs and greyhounds, and eight carts filled with English ale, pulled by teams of five horses, each ridden by (a nice touch, this) a monkey dressed in English national costume. The French king had deliberately banned villagers on the procession's route from giving the Englishmen food, so that they'd turn up in the capital looking pathetic and disheveled, but the organizer had thought of this. When they arrived in Paris, even the Parisians were impressed— 'ooh la la,' they probably said.

The display was recognition of London's newfound wealth and ostentation. From this point on, the people of the city become recognizable as the wealth-obsessed, fashion-conscious spivs that the rest of the country loves so much. A thriving trade hub, London even had its first restaurant, a twenty-four-hour 'cook-shop' by the Thames, as regular patron William FitzStephen called it, which served 'Seasonal foods, dishes roast, fried and boiled, fish of every size.' Alehouses were for the first time springing up, recognized by a long projecting pole beside the door, where a bush was hung. (Today hanging baskets are still hung outside pubs in England.)[13]

By the end of the twelfth century, England had become more prosperous than ever. There were now 150 fairs and 350 markets across the country, church spires were shooting up, wool and tin were big exports, and London was now home to thirty thousand people and second city Norwich between five and ten thousand. The twelfth and thirteenth centuries saw huge economic growth in western Europe,[14] and in England the population tripled in two hundred years, reaching six million in 1300, a figure it wouldn't reach again until the eighteenth century after the devastation of the Black Death.[15] London had also become the center of government by the time of Henry II, with the Treasury moving from Winchester to Westminster in the twelfth century, although there weren't really capital cities as such, as the royal court traveled around with the king and his entourage.

FitzStephen also described how Londoners liked nothing better than indulging in cockfights, football, dancing, 'leaping,' casting stones, and practicing 'feates of warre with disarmed launces and shields.' Wrestling was also a popular sport with rich and poor, although women weren't allowed to watch; every year there was a big wrestling match on St. Bartholomew's Day (August 24) in Clerkenwell, and back in those days it was real.

Still, not everyone was a fan; Richard of Devizes, who had come from Winchester, wrote of London in the 1190s: 'Whatever evil or malicious thing can be found anywhere in the world can also be found in that city. There are masses of pimps. You will meet more braggarts there than in the whole of France. The number of parasites is infinite. Actors, jesters, smooth-skinned lads, Moors, flat-terers, pretty boys, effeminates, pederasts, singing and dancing girls, quacks, belly-dancers, sorcerers, extortioners, night-wanderers, magicians, mimes, beggars, buffoons. If you do not wish to dwell with evil-doers, do not live in London.' What he'd have made of Soho on a Saturday night can only be guessed at.

And the city was certainly dangerous: savage dogs hung around St. Paul's cathedral terrorizing passersby until mid-thirteenth century,[16] while its murder rate would have been higher than any US urban area today, and as with all towns at the time everyone had to be home after the curfew bell was rang at 8 p.m.*

Aside from pimps, quacks, and smooth-skinned lads, a grow-ing number of men made good money as merchants. Among them was the Norman, Gilbert of Thierceville, and as Gilbert's son had become a crony of the king, so it was natural that Henry should turn to him to organize the English display in Paris. He did a brilliant job. His name was Thomas Becket, and he and Henry were to seri-ously fall out.

---

* Wallingford in Oxfordshire was alone in being allowed a later curfew, 9 p.m., as reward for the city supporting William the Conqueror in 1066.

CHAPTER THREE

Twelve Angry Men

Magna Carta was just one part of a legal revolution that took place in the twelfth and thirteenth centuries, one that was mainly carried out not by the sociopathic monarchs of the age but very clever and diligent clerics, few of whom are remembered.

When he came to the throne, Henry II fired all the country's treasurers, and then fined them for getting fired. He rehired Henry I's moneyman, Nigel, Bishop of Ely, and put him in charge of national finances: Nigel was given the new job title of Lord High Treasurer of England, a position that later sort of developed into First Lord of the Treasury (from 1714), which evolved into the role of prime minister, a position always held by churchmen during the medieval era.

Like the grandfather after whom he was named, Henry II was very concerned with good government, a necessary worry for someone in control of such a large empire that needed money. Perhaps his most groundbreaking ruling was the 1166 Assize of Clarendon, in which the king declared that the Crown would investigate all crimes, whether or not local lords were looking into them. Previously, the neighborhood bigwig would investigate any wrongdoing in the area, which gave him effective impunity (after all, he may well have committed it). Under the Assize, people could also claim back property they had inherited (*mort d'ancestor*), or reclaim homes they had been ejected from (*novel disseisin*), thereby establishing property law. Devices called tally sticks were used to register payments to the Crown, and records were kept from the twelfth to the nineteenth century by which time the technology was updated (a bonfire was made of the sticks in 1834 which, unfortunately, ended up burning down Parliament).

The Assize of Clarendon, named after the hunting lodge in Wiltshire where the king stayed, was perhaps as influential as Magna Carta in one specific way, bringing about the concept of *habeas corpus*. Meaning 'you may have the body,' this is the legal principle whereby a prisoner can report an unlawful detention before a court, the effect being that no one can be detained without due process. This is very similar to one of the key clauses of Magna Carta, and is often wrongly attributed to the charter.

Henry's most innovative change was to the way that suspects were tried. Quite reasonably, he thought that the experimental jury system used under Ethelred and his Viking successor Canute in the eleventh century was better than the two current systems of justice, either trial by ordeal or the more progressive method of trial by battle.

Trial by ordeal had been around since Saxon times, and involved the accused having to walk over the sharp bit of a plow after it had first been put in a fire to make it red-hot. A variation of the theme had the poor accused holding two hot irons and walking nine paces, then waiting a week to see if the wounds had healed; under this scientific method if they had recovered, the suspect was not guilty, but if the wounds had festered then they were hanged. The genius of the system was that if they had not healed then the accused would probably die in agony anyway of some horrible infection.

Alternatively, you could opt for trial by either drowning or boiling—obviously both had their downsides.

The Assize of Clarendon laid down the rules for the ordeal of cold water, stating that it was to be held in a twenty-by-twelve-foot pit outside a church. Although horrific, around four out of five people could survive the ordeal, according to modern research, assuming they were not grossly obese, something few in the medieval era would have to worry about. As long as you took a deep breath beforehand you had a reasonable chance of staying below water, and being found not guilty.

The Assize stated that if the defendant failed by floating to the top, 'he must lose one of his feet, and in this maimed condition abjure the realm.' Finding a job overseas in the twelfth century was hard at the best of times, but when most labor was physical, doing so after having been 'defooted' must have been challenging.[1] But this was obviously considered overly indulgent and so ten years later, at the Assize of Northampton, it was ruled that the guilty man should also lose his right hand.[2]

However, the law was updated once again to state that 'if the accused were men of very bad reputation, even if they succeeded in the ordeal, they must leave the country and be accounted as outlaws.' So you couldn't really win.

These trials, however, were great fun for the local community, for whom 'the ordeal by iron or water was an orchestrated religious drama, signaled by their priest's blessing of pit or iron.'[3] By Henry II's time it had become something of an event, with spectators watching the event while sipping at specially blessed water and kissing the cross. Those who wanted to attend were expected to fast 'and abstain from their wives during the night'; the accused were also made to eat nothing for three days except bread, salt, and some herbs before they had to plunge their arms into boiling water.

Trial by ordeal was killed off by those spoilsports, the Catholic Church. In 1215 at the Fourth Lateran Council, the Church banned priests from taking part in such events, and since prayers and blessings were required for the event to go ahead this effectively put it to an end.[4] The theological argument was that it was not reasonable to demand divine intervention, as if God was just a genie who could be summoned, because a miracle had to be a free act of God. However, the underlying reason was that the Church didn't like violence, and phased it out where it could.* The Church did this despite the loss it suffered as a result; priests were paid pretty good fees for ordeals and many churches owned ordeal pits and consecrated irons, so these events made them the center of the community.[5]

The Normans, meanwhile, had a pretty basic idea of divine justice: if you beat people in battle, God was on your side and therefore you were the goodie. They, therefore, introduced trial by battle, which is fairly self-explanatory. If someone committed a crime against you, you reported it and then fought them in a duel to the death; although such fights were often between fellow criminals who had turned evidence against each other. Dualists fought 'with clubs and shields, teeth and nails until one or other cried "craven."' And 'if they break their weapons . . . they must fight with their hands, firsts, nails, teeth, feet, and legs.'[6]

Knights battled with swords and lances, peasants used staves with iron heads, while women and priests could appoint a champion, which must have been hugely welcome news to men returning from a hard day's labor in the field only to discover they had to do combat with the next-door neighbor's husband. In one recorded incident from Gloucester in 1221, the ordeal ended with the loser being castrated and his testicles thrown to a group of boys, who gleefully played football with them. This particular legal case, involving two old friends called George and Thomas, had begun four years earlier. Thomas had once slept with George's wife before they were

---

*   Although the twelfth century was not ideal, compared to just two hundred years earlier, during the period of 'feudal anarchy' in which lords were at almost constant war with one another and before the Church had installed 'the truce of God,' it was paradise.

married, and there was tension in their friendship; the two were drinking one day and on the way home, while heavily drunk, George hit Thomas over the head with a stick. Thomas hit him back with an axe. Then George raised the hue and cry, whereby every man in the local area, the hundred, was expected to form a 'posse' to track down a wrongdoer. It was another four years before the authorities got around to ruling that it should be resolved by battle. Thomas lost, but in an act of liberal decadence the judges spared his life and instead ruled that he could be let off with castration and having his eyes gouged out instead. This was done by George's family 'which, supervised by court officials, they did with enthusiasm.'

Trial by ordeal was formally abolished in 1219. Trial by battle lasted into the following century, but remained in theory on the statute books, forgotten about until one murder suspect invoked it in 1818. Legal experts had to look it up and realized he was right, and the man got off; afterwards Parliament quickly got rid of it.[7]

In 1179, Henry II allowed defendants to decide whether they wanted trial by battle or the case decided by a group of twelve local knights, a privilege described then as 'a royal benefit granted to the people by the clemency of the prince on the advice of the magnates.' Or as we now call it, the jury system.

Juries had developed from a tradition in Anglo-Saxon England whereby people had to bring a group of men, often twelve, to act as character witnesses. This evolved into the idea that officials had to gather a dozen local men to give their opinion on the suspect's character and decide what the threadbare evidence suggested (today of course juries are supposed to judge purely on the evidence, and to ignore previous crimes). The related system of grand juries, whereby a group of people were brought to hear whether there was enough evidence to try someone, date from the reign of the hopeless Ethelred the Unready around the turn of the millennium, and lasted until the nineteenth century in England; they are still used in the United States.

The new nonviolent trials by jury became known as assizes, from the Norman French *asise*, to sit. Elsewhere in Europe trial by ordeal was replaced with the more forward-looking trial by torture (of both accused and witnesses)—only England and Denmark took the jury route.

Strangely, as the law became fairer and more moral, it also became more severe. Men could no longer just pay compensation as in the good old days, but were treated as sinners who should expect to be punished. Before 1066, the punishment for forgery was to have a hand cut off, but it was increased to having a hand cut off with castration by 1200, and the following century it had become a capital offense. There was also a crude idea that punishments should fit the crime: arsonists were burned to death, rapists were castrated, and people convicted of slander or false accusation had their tongue cut out.

But generally speaking justice was corrupt and a wealthy man, accused of a crime, could offer money 'for having the king's love,' or that 'the king's anger might be relaxed.'[8]

Alternatively, you could stay in jail until you opted for a trial, although prisons were pretty rough, and it was later decreed that 'a defendant who opted for jail should suffer *peine forte et dure* from heavy stones placed on his chest until he either chose to go to trial or was pressed to death.' So that rather ruled out that option; instead two-thirds chose to flee and become outlaws.[9]

Under Henry there was a large increase in the number of judges and legally trained staff; and growing demand for the use of courts once people learned they could sue each other. The new legal staff wrote documents called 'Final Concords,' which set out in a semiofficial way the terms of court settlements, in Latin, although even then men complained it was a sort of legalese Latin that people who understood the language couldn't get their heads around. In this way, in English (and American) law the interpretation by one judge sets a precedent for what others decide. Court reports, or rolls, were kept for the first time, although a relatively small number survive. It was a mixture of different traditions, and in the words of historian Robert Tombs: 'The English Common Law was the first national system of law in Europe. It was a hybrid of Anglo-Saxon and Norman customs and Roman theories, using French terms and concepts—debt, contract, heir, trespass, court, judge, jury—and (until 1731) keeping records in Latin.'[10]

In order to bring criminals to justice there grew up regular judicial tours of the country by the king's judges, or sometimes just the king's friends, who went around dispensing said justice.[11] The principle of a traveling circuit was that, unlike local judges, they would not know anyone and therefore be impartial. Meanwhile, royal officials meeting in Westminster Hall became known as the Bench, later called the Court of Common Pleas. Previously, much justice was done privately, either by local lords or even by individuals—with mixed results. In Bedfordshire, for example, in the 1170s a man got his next-door neighbor convicted of stealing from his house, and did the blinding and castrating himself. Later, it turned out the neighbor was innocent. In 1194, the office of coroner was established to record serious offenses in each county, and by the time of Edward I in 1272, blood money could no longer be used, and the distinction between criminal and civil law also emerged fully.

Henry II also ordered that jails be built in every county. Perhaps the most famous was the Clink prison, set up in the twelfth century under the authority of the bishop of Winchester in Southwark, and which became slang for jails in general. The diocese of Winchester owned huge amounts of land in the area, which faced London on the opposite bank of the Thames and was outside of the city's jurisdiction; this included a number of brothels, a strange situation that was still around in Shakespeare's time and is mentioned in one play. Prison was not a great place back then, and deaths were very common; in one year, half of all cases of deaths recorded in the Coroners

Rolls for the City of London involved men who expired in jail, and considering the number of free people in London at the time who died from misadventurer, murder, and various other unnatural causes this must have been a lot.[12]

William of Newburgh said that under the king 'a virgin could walk from one end of the realm to the other with her bosom full of gold and come to no harm.' That is clearly not true, but Henry II left a huge legacy, and for inventing the jury system he was honored by the British people in 2002 by being voted the ninetieth most important Briton, thirteen places below Robbie Williams from Take That.[13]

But the king's expansion of power would also have an influence on the barons when his demented son took over; after all, if all subjects had to be held accountable, why not the king? And yet, despite all this, there were one group of people Henry couldn't bring to justice.

CHAPTER FOUR

A Lowborn Cleric

Priests, meanwhile, were made to go through a different type of ordeal, having to stand in front of a church altar and eat a slice of cheese on consecrated bread. If they were guilty, the clergy argued, God would intervene and stop them from swallowing; you can see why the Church didn't have any trouble recruiting at the time.

It rather goes without saying that during this period the Catholic Church held enormous power in western Europe, and kings were wise to keep it on side; and the respect shown by royalty was generally not just cynical politics. Henry II was a devout man, despite his fidgeting during Mass, and when he swore on his eyes, he expected to go blind if he broke his oath. Significantly, Clause 1 of Magna Carta starts by stating 'that the English Church shall be free, and shall have its rights undiminished, and its liberties unimpaired.' For central to the conflict of this age was the relationship between the Plantagenet monarchs and the only being more powerful—the Almighty.

Under the Normans, the Holy See had gained greater control over English affairs, but even back in Anglo-Saxon times the Crown had been obliged to hand over an annual fee to Rome, called 'Peter's Pence' (after the first Pope, St. Peter). The Church was more than just a religious institution, and rather like a government in itself. It ran vast areas of life that the state would now consider its problem: schools, hospitals and relief of the poor especially. And, unlike the staid world of the Crown, where positions were inherited and only changed hands at the point of a sword, the Church accepted men of all backgrounds. Within it, a man could even rise up the social ranks, providing he had a decent education, although admittedly finding a good school in the catchment area was a difficult task for the typical twelfth-century serf. Among the great clerics of the time, many had come from poor families, such as Robert Grosseteste ('big head'), who grew up in Herefordshire and went onto become Bishop of Lincoln; Grosseteste is widely credited with introducing the idea of the controlled experiment into western science. However, wealthy families often ensured one of their own got a prize job; an illegitimate son of Henry II became Archbishop of York, the number two position in the English Church.

But all this power made the clergy unpopular to some, especially as everyone was expected to hand over a share of their income—a tithe (literally, tenth)—to the Church, a payment that was routinely avoided, and by many accounts considered socially acceptable to do so.

And, human nature being what it is, sometimes the clergy didn't live up to their own exacting standards. Monks denied themselves meat, as they were supposed to, but they had started to define this as only freshly cut meat from the bone; therefore, bacon was technically sort of okay, and they could also eat 'umbles,' sheep entrails like heart and liver cooked in bread crumbs. (Since this was considered far inferior to other dishes, someone forced to eat 'umble pie' was seen as suffering an inferior position.) Monks were also only allowed wine on feast days, although every third day was a feast day, so they could still easily consume well above the government recommended daily limits and keep their vows.

In one instance, when the shrine to St. Edmund at Bury was damaged and the Abbot blamed the monks for their gluttony, he suggested they should cut back on the food and save money to spend on restorations. They suggested that St. Edmund could restore his own shrine without their help. Indeed, the stereotype of the chubby friar is fairly accurate, as research on monk skeletons from three London monasteries showed that they were five times as likely as the population as a whole to get obesity-related joint diseases; over 11 percent of those buried at Eynsham Abbey in Oxfordshire had 'DISH' a condition related to being overweight.[1]

Popular cynicism about the clergy is reflected in a style of poem of the time, known as a *fabliaux*, which often had a bawdy theme. One such song told the story of a bishop who finds a 'sparkling, jeweled ring' on the road and takes it only to find it gives him an uncontrolled erection that breaks out of his clothes and drags along the ground. The *fabliaux* were filled with rude words such as *vit, coilles, con, cul,* and *foutre*, which you'll only understand if you listen to French hip-hop.

Some clerics were quite bawdy, and in the words of one historian: 'The parish priest was often grossly illiterate, with scarcely enough Latin to repeat the church services correctly; he was shockingly ill-paid, and was driven to take money for Masses and other spiritual offices to supplement his meager income.' Priests often married or 'kept a hearth-girl in his house who kindled his fire but extinguished his virtue.'[2]

Some, however, did live by the rule of celibacy, whatever the cost. In 1114, Thomas, Archbishop of York, was seriously ill, and at the time it was generally believed that sex was vital for health, so the doctors recommended he take a woman and told him God would understand as it was for his health.[3] They provided him with a room and an 'attractive' young lady, but in the morning when they examined his urine they (somehow) deduced that he hadn't actually done the deed and he admitted he had only gone into the room with her so as not to hurt their feelings.[4] The archbishop told them he'd rather die than break the vow of chastity—which he did. Although a chronicle praised Thomas's great virtue, he was actually unwell because he had become morbidly obese, so the sex might have killed him anyway.

Churchmen were not always that meek, however. In 1176, a dispute over who was senior between the Archbishop of Canterbury and Archbishop of York—a long-running argument—ended in 'fists, sticks, and clubs.' Likewise, many viewed them as being overpaid and with overlarge entourages, similar to the criticism leveled at politicians and public sector officials today. In recognition of this, Archbishop Hubert Walter published a decree in 1179 that limited the number of retainers an archbishop could have to just fifty men, and thirty for a bishop.[5]

The Church's rules against working on holy days also caused resentment. One story from the twelfth century has a Londoner being reproached by a priest for laboring on the feast of St. Erkenwald, an obscure figure who most people even then had never heard of. The man replied, in a tirade that sounds like something from modern talk radio: 'You lot grow fat and soft with idleness, you don't have a real job, your life is just a game or a play . . . You clerics with your everlasting useless dirges despise us, though we are the ones who do all the real work. And then you go and bring in some Erkenwald or other to justify your idleness. When we've made a bit of money then we have a holiday, and a good time dancing and singing. You keep your festivals, your mouldy old tunes and your Erkenwald to yourselves. Leave us alone.'[6] According to the canon at St. Paul's who recounted this tirade, the man ranting about Erkenwald then staggered under the weight of timber he was carrying, tripped over a half-buried skull that happened to be lying in the churchyard and was fatally injured. Well, perhaps.

Despite our image of medieval people living in a world of superstition, abject terror, and haunting Gregorian chants, there was also a surprising amount of nonbelief. Peter of Cornwall, prior of Holy Trinity, Aldgate, complained in 1200: 'There are many people who do not believe that God exists, nor do they think that the human soul lives on after the death of the body. They consider that the universe has always been as it is now and is ruled by chance rather than providence.'

The king wasn't among them, but the biggest problem, as far as he was concerned, was the 'Benefit of Clergy,' whereby churchmen were tried in religious rather than state courts. Although the earliest surviving record of clerical trials suggests that a large proportion of these were for sex offenses, this does not mean it was a land populated by amorous Friar Tuck-types feasting on ale and ogling wenches, since most of these wrongdoers weren't even priests. Technically a cleric included anyone in Minor Orders, including clerks, doctors and lawyers, and almost any literate person with some position in the church, many of which were part-time or semi-official. So they weren't necessarily men of the cloth, just those who worked for the institution, who were expected to shave the crown of their head and renounce facial hair, colorful clothes, weapons, and pubs. All of these people could claim Benefit of Clergy, the right to be tried by a Church court, and by the end of the thirteenth century, some forty thousand ordained men were across England, one in twenty-five of the adult male population.[7]

Besides which, detailed study has found that most people who claimed Benefit of Clergy weren't actually clerics, with as few as 24 percent being genuine in the later Middle Ages.[8] The plea evolved so that eventually anyone able to show proof of literacy could use it to reduce their punishment, and even as late as 1613 it cropped up when two men were convicted of burgling the Earl of Sussex's house. The judge passed down his sentence: 'the said Paul reads, to be branded; the said William does not read, to be hanged.'[9] Fifteen years earlier, the playwright Ben Jonson had used the technicality to escape serious punishment after killing a man in a duel in Hoxton. The part of the Bible people were expected to recite—Psalm 51— therefore became known as 'the neck verse' because it would save you from hanging. Benefit of Clergy was last used in 1827, although it could no longer be applied for serious offenses from the sixteenth century.[10]

There had been some one hundred murders by clerics during the reign of Henry but there were four especially scandalous cases that angered the king, among them one of a man in Worcestershire who had raped a girl and stabbed her father; all he received was lifelong penance in a monastery, which outraged public opinion. Despite such deplorable cases of injustice, Pope Gregory VIII said that clergy were immune to layman's law, and so they could not be prosecuted in ordinary courts.

Part of the problem were the low standards for qualification to the Church. Since clergy who had committed a crime mostly just got a penance, this 'had no terror for the disreputable multitude of persons who, without occupation or scruple, swelled the lower ranks of the profession,' since there was a very low bar for joining the clergy in terms of education or character. 'Scandals were frequent; crimes were committed almost with impunity.'[11]

Henry had a different view to the Pope on the relationship between Church and state. When the Bishop of Chichester said in his presence that only the Pontiff could hire and fire bishops, Henry replied: 'Quite right, a bishop can't be deposed,' and then, gesturing with his hands, added, 'but he can be ejected with a good shove.' The king once sent a note to the monks of St. Swithin's Priory, stating: 'I order you to hold a free election; nevertheless, I forbid you to elect anyone save Richard, my clerk.'

The impunity of clerics was a big problem for the king, but he thought he could solve it through cronyism. Thomas Becket was about the least likely person to be put in charge of the Church, being a *nouveau riche* merchant's son with brains and ambition. He had become a knight and then a clerk, his financial skills helping him climb the corporate ladder, and he also did well financially out of Henry's various small wars on the continent. Like any cockney—the word, from the term 'cock eggs' (i.e., rotten eggs), emerged in late medieval times—Becket was extremely flash about his appearance, wearing the finest clothes and jewelry; he even kept a pet monkey and some wolves, which he trained to hunt other wolves. During the 1158 Paris trip, Becket's private wardrobe contained twenty-four changes of silk robes,[12] and when he became archbishop he had an entourage of fifty-two clerks working for him.

Through his work Becket had become the king's boozing pal, though their friendship had a macho rivalry to it that, were it shown in a gangster film, would obviously suggest things would end violently. They were once seen wrestling over Becket's coat as the royal carriage went through London, after he had pointed out a poor man's coatless condition and the king suggested he give him his. The king won, but then kings tended to.

So when Archbishop Tedbald of Canterbury died in 1161, Henry could think of no one better suited to the job of leading the nation's spiritual health than his old cockney wheeler-dealer friend. Becket was quickly ordained a priest, and the following day he was made archbishop.

But if Henry thought he would have a pliant yes-man working for him, he was sadly mistaken—for his worldly buddy turned into a bigger pain than previous archbishops. To the king's fury, Becket refused to allow clerics to be tried like laymen, and this came to a head in 1163 when Philip de Broc, the Canon of Bedford, was accused of murdering a knight. After he was acquitted at the Bishop of Lincoln's court and brought to a lay court, the canon refused to recognize the secular court and laid at the judge 'distressing insults, and many abuses' that the official Simon Fitz Peter reported to the king.[13]

Becket would not help try the cleric, and he had also begun to show disturbing signs of actually taking the job seriously, shouting 'whoremonger' at the king's assistant (who, to be fair, was a sort of pimp, his job being to find his boss mistresses), and publicly disavowing luxury.* He also protected clerical privileges, and was known to allow his archdeacons to accept fines rather than give a penance, a system that is quite obviously going to be exploited.

It did not help that the king's circle was quite seedy. Henry's court was described as being filled with 'actors, singers, dicers, confectioners, huxters, gamblers, buffoons, barbers.'[14] Walter Map said the courtiers of Henry were 'creatures of the night' and 'who leave nothing untouched and untried.' One courtier described life at court as Hell, filled with 'the foul trailings of worms [and] serpents, and all manner of creeping things.'

In contrast, the new saintly Becket even started wearing a rough goat's hair shirt infected with lice, a sign of extreme piety and, stranger still, began to walk around with a massive crucifix around his neck. Becket's enormous ego grew larger, a condition reflected in his personal copy of the Bible, which had a picture of himself below that of Christ. The king's cunning plan had completely backfired.

With their relationship in tatters, the archbishop attempted to leave England in 1164, leading Henry to ask 'Don't you think the country is big enough to hold both of us?' But later that year the king expelled him, and Becket spent the next six years in France, no longer on speaking terms with his old friend and with no sign of reconciliation in the air. Becket must have had an inkling that it would not be a happy ending; in November 1166, he dreamed that four

---

*   Whether Becket was a true believer or not, we cannot tell, for he said Mass very quickly, 'according to his friend and biographer Herbert of Bosham . . . to minimize the skeptical thoughts that tended to trouble him at that point.'

knights were murdering him and, as they say, sometimes dreams do come true.

Becket tried to resign by throwing the ring of office at Pope Alexander III but he returned it; being Archbishop of Canterbury really was the impossible job. Henry also banished or imprisoned Becket's friends and relatives. Overall there were twelve peace talks over the years 1164–1170. On one occasion, Becket annoyed his opponents by making a point of arriving while carrying a full-sized cross, the kind of histrionics that really got on everyone's nerves.[15]

While intermediaries tried to bring the two together, the king grew impatient; in 1170 he needed an archbishop nearby because he was desperate for his eldest son, Henry, to be crowned (wary of what happened when Henry I died, the king wanted his heir ready as coruler). The king made the Archbishop of York, England's second most senior priest, do the honors, and he blocked all ports so that any disapproving message from the Pope couldn't reach him (similar to putting your fingers in your ears and shouting 'la-la-la,' but on a very large scale).

When the two enemies met on July 22, 1170, at the ill-named site of Traitor's Field by the Loire, they hugged and made up. But then Henry told Becket about the coronation performed without him, and the archbishop exploded in a rage, his mood worsened by the extremely uncomfortable hair shirt underwear he now insisted on wearing as a mark of holiness.

Becket returned to England later that year, The evening before crossing the channel he excommunicated the Archbishop of York and eight other bishops present at the coronation of the younger Henry. And on Christmas Day 1170, he again slammed the king from the pulpit of Canterbury Cathedral, throwing a candle to the floor and saying of those who had taken part in the coronation: 'May they be damned by Jesus Christ!'

When he heard this, Henry was naturally furious and went on one of his many rants, but he never said, 'Who will rid me of this turbulent priest?' as he is commonly misquoted. What he actually shouted was the much angrier: 'What miserable drones and traitors have I nourished and promoted in my household, who let their lord be treated with such shameful contempt by a lowborn cleric?' Four young knights in attendance, eager to impress the boss, rode to the Channel to confront Becket at Canterbury. The men, led by Reginald FitzUrse ('son of a bear'), were severely hungover by the time they arrived in England the following day, and having picked up another twelve men on the way, they were pumped up for a fight.

When they arrived at the cathedral, Becket, with characteristic tact and diplomacy, shouted 'Pimp!' at FitzUrse. Insults were traded, and the ensuing horseplay had obviously gotten way out of control by the time one of the knights sliced off the top of Becket's head, his blood and brains spilling all over the cathedral floor. 'That escalated quickly,' as the saying goes.

Understandably, the nation was shocked. Archbishops weren't supposed to be murdered, especially not in cathedrals, and by the king's men. Everyone had turned against Becket in the end, and before he died the bishops of York, London, and Salisbury had gone to Normandy to complain to the king about his conduct. Now, however, not a word could be said against him.

Rather than going to ground for a couple of months and then reappearing in public to say he was 'battling his demons' or citing his father's lack of love, in those days public figures who messed up were expected to wear sackcloth and have themselves whipped in public, which is exactly what the king did at Canterbury Cathedral—five from each of the dozen bishops in attendance and three from each of the eighty monks. (Although Henry's beating was probably symbolic, as otherwise that many would have killed him.)[16]

The murderers were sent off to the Holy Land to do penance, a virtual death sentence anyway, and FitzUrse died soon after. The

king was also ordered to go to Jerusalem, but after repeated promises and procrastination, eventually the matter was dropped.*

The murder was major news across Europe; the French king Philip
immediately tried to exploit it, urging the Pope to 'draw the sword of
St. Peter,' in other words, excommunicate Henry and allow the French
to invade his land with impunity. The Pope didn't buy it. And the day
after Henry was flogged, his army captured King William the Lion of
Scotland, who was taken 'shackled under the belly of a horse,' and this
was seen as divine judgment. God was okay with him.

Becket was quickly made a saint, to the smirking cynicism of
his contemporaries. His main enemies, the bishops of London and
York, who'd long wished him dead, took the lead roles in his canon-
ization. 'An ass he always was, and an ass he'll always be,' was the
Bishop of London's strictly off-the-record view.

Soon after the killing of Becket, the people of Canterbury began
pouring into the cathedral, cutting off bits of their clothes and dip-
ping them in the archbishop's blood, anointing their eyes with the
fluid; others brought vessels to capture the blood.

And whether he deserved his sainthood, and whatever effect the
murder had on the roles of church and state, it certainly turned
Canterbury into a first-rate tourist resort, with every sort of Becket
gimmick now on sale, including Canterbury Water, a mixture of
regular water and the saint's blood. This 'Becket Water,' as it was
also known, was supposed to cure blindness and heal cripples, and
was manufactured on a large scale with an inscription in Latin: 'All
weakness and pain is removed, the healed man eats and drinks,
and evil and death pass away.' If it didn't work, it was because the
person wasn't sufficiently pious.[17] There were also T-shaped badges

---

*   One of the killers, Hugh de Morville, was supposedly of evil heritage.
As an example of this evil apparently his mother was so overcome by
passion for a young man that she had him boiled to death when he
spurned her advances.

showing Thomas on a ship returning from exile, as well as a badge of dubious taste depicting the sword that killed him.

All sorts of miracles were attributed to the site: there was 'Mad Henry' of Forthwick, who came out of the tomb sane; a blind woman who touched her handkerchief into the martyr's bloody eyes and dabbed it on to her own, restoring her sight; and another blind woman who, while visiting the shrine, was run over by yet another blind person on horseback and had her eyesight restored after praying to Becket (no one commented on the fact that a blind man was allowed to wander the kingdom on a horse).

So, tragic though Becket's death was, it was a huge boost for the city's tourism industry, which now vied with some of Europe's top religious sites as a center for mystical nicknacks. You couldn't buy that sort of publicity. Even though demented radical Protestants destroyed most of the cheap souvenirs four centuries later, forty-five boxes of the archbishop's relics are still floating around today.

As a result of the killing, the Church basically won, the clergy securing their immunities until the Reformation, when Henry VIII took a new and fresh approach by just beheading anyone who disagreed with him.

Another bonus was that as a penitence Henry commissioned a new stone bridge in London, which was completed in 1209 and stood until 1831, during which time it witnessed countless disasters. In 1281–82 five arches just collapsed and floated downstream when 'there was such a frost and snow, as no man living could remember the like,' and the only reason the Great Fire of London of 1666 did not spread south of the river is that a third of London Bridge had been burned down in another fire thirty years earlier.

Ireland

While Henry's conflict with Becket affects few people outside of the Kent tourist board, his other major blunder is still with us. For the Anglo-Saxons, Ireland never really appeared on the radar except as a place for noblemen to hide after they'd murdered someone in a drunken fight. But now the Normans were in charge, and if you lived next door to a Norman the chances were that when you came back home from work he'd have built a castle over your house, made your wife his serf, and demanded you work on his back garden twice a week. In fact, when he was very young Henry II had wanted to conquer Ireland for his youngest brother William but his mother persuaded him not to.

But now the Normans invaded, half-supported in this venture by the Catholic Church, which did not approve of the Irish Church's lax attitude to sexual matters, especially divorce, concubines, and illegitimacy, which were all still rife. The Normans, despite being ferocious maniacs, were also very pious on such matters, and thought the Irish to be sexual deviants; the Norman chronicler Gerald of Wales visited the country with King John and noted while there he heard about a goat having sexual relations with a woman: 'how unworthy and unspeakable' he wrote about it, extensively. Whether or not this was true we can't tell; Gerald also claimed a similar thing about the French, this time involving a lion, so it seems to have been a running theme with him.

It all began in 1170 when an Irish chieftain, Diarmaid MacMurchada of Leinster, lost his kingdom to a rival warlord and turned for help from Richard Fitzgilbert, Earl of Pembroke—just about the worst person for invite to your country. The De Clare family, from which Fitzgilbert came, already owned twenty towns on the Welsh border and were famously belligerent even compared to other Normans. 'Strongbow,' as the earl was called, soon overstayed his welcome by conquering Dublin and Waterford, where he ordered that seventy local residents have their legs broken and then chucked in the sea. Anglo-Irish relations were off to a shaky start.

Henry was extremely suspicious of Strongbow, and invaded the following year to keep an eye on him—eight centuries later, the English might admit that they suffered from what military euphemism types call 'mission creep.' There was another reason, though: in the past, Ireland had been used as a base by Viking raiders who established a kingdom there, many a miserable Anglo-Saxon ending up in the Dublin slave market, and Henry didn't want some of his wilder barons to set up shop over there and potentially threaten him. And so a local dispute between warlords escalated into centuries of colonialism, one Britain is still trying to make up for by awarding its neighbor twelve points every year at the Eurovision Song Contest.

But Henry also had another motive: his vast empire had already been parceled out among his three elder sons, and the youngest, John, had no kingdom to call his own. Fighting the most militaristic people in Europe, the Irish didn't stand a chance against the Anglo-Norman 'grey foreigners,' so-called because of their chainmail armor. Henry's army soon took control of the area around Dublin, and this English colony became known as 'the Pale,' from the Latin for stake or boundary (so giving us the expression whereby anything outside was 'beyond the pale'). He then gave Ireland to John as a consolation prize.

CHAPTER FIVE

The War without Love

For all the problems that the Irish invasion was to cause, it didn't stop any of Henry's family troubles. The king's four sons were like medieval playboys, blessed with superhuman arrogance, violent tempers, and enormous kingdom-sized trust funds, and they would ultimately all turn against their father, in what became known as 'the war without love.' Also pitted against the permanently furious monarch was his wife Eleanor, whom Henry called 'his hated queen' and whom he ended up having imprisoned for fifteen years. It was all part of the family tradition: back in 1156, Henry had crushed a rebellion by his younger brother, another Geoffrey, and his sons and grandsons would also end up fighting, betraying, and killing one another.

His eldest, called 'Henry the Young King,' was a dashing figure who, at the time, was considered the pinnacle of chivalry. He was a star of jousting tournaments, or tourneys, which were now in their heyday, having begun in eleventh-century France as a way for knights to amuse themselves, train for war, win armor, and generally hang out. Rulers were nervous about tourneys because they led to conspiracies, and Henry II and Henry III both tried to ban them, while the Church didn't like the violence and refused burial to men who participated, saying they would languish in hell, forever, in burning armor—but this didn't seem to deter the endless supply of aristocratic young men keen for a fight.

However, the Vatican abandoned this stand in 1316, when Pope John XXII decided they were good training for crusaders (although the Crusades were effectively lost by now anyway). And to start with, they were very violent indeed, essentially huge melees held out in the countryside with very high casualty rates. By the year 1300, they had become less ferocious and more regulated—Richard the Lionheart established the first permanent venues—and by the following century had evolved into what we would now imagine, with two pointy-helmeted knights charging at each other with a lance and trying to win the favor of hefty-bosomed maidens. But in Henry's time they were essentially organized hooligan meetings with horses and weapons, no more romantic than a bunch of West Ham and Millwall fans fighting in a parking lot.

The tournaments were there to extol chivalry, a concept that began around the turn of the millennium in Germany and France and was originally a sort of cult of violence among bored aristocratic men with nothing else to do; however, with pressure from the Church, chivalry also developed into a set of rules regarding the treatment of prisoners, at first just fellow aristocrats but eventually women and children. Chivalry idealized a sort of perfect warrior, the *preudhomme* or 'best kind of man,' who had all the qualities knights should display, being 'skilled in combat and courageous, faithful, wise and able to give good counsel, but also canny, even wily, in war when necessary.'[1] The opposite of the *preudhomme* was the *losengiers*, the serpent-tongued deceivers.

The great chivalry handbook *Le livre de chevalerie*, written in the fourteenth century by Geoffrey de Charny, suggests for the first time that knights look after the poor and treat women in a nice way.

Knights had many traditions that still echo today. Among them was dubbing, from the French *adouber*, to arm, which meant giving someone a weapon, usually a belt. The dubbing would be followed by the *collee*, a form of ritualized beating, which eventually evolved into the modern custom of knighthood where the monarch taps one's shoulder with a sword (a form of dubbing is carried out in some modern gangs). Knights for hire were known as 'free lances,' while another word also common for journalists, 'a hack,' comes from the sort of packhorse used at the time. (It came to mean someone who would do anything for a meal.)

Tournaments, by the standards of twenty-first-century sport, were absurdly dangerous: one year in Germany, eighty knights were killed in one game, and this wasn't that exceptional. Among the sports seen at the tournament was cudgeling, which was won when blood poured down the opponent's scalp; quarterstaff, in which poles over six feet long were used to hit and knock the opponent over, preferably out. Or singlestick, similar to quarterstaff but which ended when one of the chaps was covered in blood. In the twelfth century there were mock battles and brute force was the important factor, but two hundred years later there were two horsemen, and skill was important. There were also far fewer fatalities by this point, although still many, and the barriers between the two knights weren't introduced until the fifteenth century.

Tourneys attracted all sorts of entertainers and craftsmen, something like a modern music festival. Heraldry also evolved at this time, so that people could know who they were fighting in the orgy of violence; eventually these standards became attached to the families involved.

Tourneys also attracted ladies, who would present prizes after the men had approached them and bowed, presumably half beaten to death by this point. Then the woman would announce, as recorded on one occasion, that 'the seide ladyes and gentilwomen seyen that ye, Sir—have done the best joust this day. Therefore the seide ladyes and gentilwomen gevyn you this diamonde and send you much worship and joy of your lady.'

Sometimes, of course, the ladies were the prize, and chivalry often encouraged lots of men to do really stupid things in order to show off in front of women. In the 1330s, for example, some English knights went to France wearing eye patches, 'having sworn to ladies at court that they would not open one of their eyes until victory was achieved. . . . Needless to say, thus encumbered, most died as a result,' as one historian puts it.[2]

Chivalry would reach its peak with the book *Le Morte d'Arthur,* the romantic glamorization of the mythical British king of Camelot fame; it was published in 1485, as the medieval world was fading in the face of printing and gunpowder (feudalism depended on a lord controlling a castle, which were of little use against cannons). Much of what we understand of chivalric attitudes come from this story, written by Sir Thomas Malory, who was technically a knight although his own life didn't quite live up to the ideal; he was convicted of breaking and entering, extortion, and two counts of rape during a colorful career.

Arthur was considered the ideal monarch as far back as the twelfth century, having been largely created in Oxford—at the very same time as the Empress Matilda was escaping in the snow—by a clergyman called Geoffrey of Monmouth. His book, *Historia Regum Britanniae,* or History of the Kings of Britain, was enormously influential, but as one twentieth century historian rather kindly put it, 'Geoffrey's work is not pure history.'[3]

The two other historians of the period, Henry of Huntingdon and William of Malmesbury, at least tried to keep their stories within the boundaries of possibility, but Geoffrey's were far more popular. He borrowed a tale that had been taken back to France by knights visiting Cornwall in 1113; the locals told the Frenchmen about a heroic king who had fought for their people centuries ago against the invading Saxons, a king who had never died and would one day come back and sort everything out. The French knights obviously didn't think much of it, as they laughed in the local peoples' faces, and were pelted with vegetables, but the story of King Arthur became a big hit in France.

It started a boom in legend: around the same time a story sprang up about Joseph of Arimathea—the Biblical character who helped bury Jesus—visiting Glastonbury, and a subplot developed whereby Christ himself spent his missing years in ancient Britain. The lyrics to *Jerusalem*, written in 1804 by William Blake, borrow from this myth with the words 'Did those feet in ancient times, walk on England's mountains green?'[4] (The short answer is: no.)

Arthur was so popular that Henry III's brother Richard spent huge amounts on a castle at Tintagel in Cornwall that had 'no strategic or domestic benefits' whatsoever but was where Geoffrey of Monmouth claimed Arthur had been conceived.[5]

Not everyone was caught up by this, however; the Yorkshire monk William of Newburgh stated at the time of Geoffrey's story that 'everything that man wrote about Arthur and his successors, and indeed his predecessors, was made up!' However, Geoffrey's work was the second bestselling book of the time, after the Bible, so maybe Newburgh was just bitter.

The Arthurian legend helped form an idea of what a king should be, an ideal that would certainly help articulate criticism of King John. But it also encouraged a sort of ruinous economic policy; in the stories, Arthur is always absurdly generous to his men, granting an infinite supply of largesse, and there was a real-life parallel—the king's son Henry, who was the very epitome of chivalry and also an irresponsible spendthrift.

Despite being crowned joint monarch in 1170, Henry the Young King had been a frustrated pawn in his father's power game his entire life. Bizarrely, and against all Church rules, he had been married since the age of five, to the King of France's two-year-old daughter Margaret; this might seem somewhat on the young side, and even at the time people thought it very odd, but the Pope agreed to it, as he needed Henry's help in a war against the Byzantines.

The two children were married in 1160 in the presence of a pair of cardinals, and as a result the Plantagenet king gained the Vexin, a disputed region in France.

Henry II had been taught by his mother Matilda that the way to engineer loyalty was to deny favor, for 'an unruly hawk' could only be tamed if made hungry; this was the tactic he used to turn his young sons into grateful and loyal children and it failed spectacularly.

As a young man, Henry the Young King had also been attached to Thomas Becket, in whose household he had been partly raised, and fell out with his father as a result. This was apparently one motive for the disastrous rebellion that followed.

Young Henry had an enormous entourage that cost £200 per day, at a time when the royal income for a county would be £200 a *year.* On one occasion he held a celebration of 'great magnificence' just for his friends called William—110 of them. One account of the time asks: 'It was a source of wonder where the wealth was to be found.' In fact it wasn't, as it was soon running out. This kind of luxurious extravagance was great in fairy tales but unsustainable in real life, and probably didn't suggest to his father he would be the wisest of rulers.

Although considered the epitome of manliness in England, Henry the Young King's band of knights were also perennially beaten at tourneys on the continent, and 'never came to a single tournament site without being humiliated and ill-used,' a long running English sporting tradition.[6]

Among the most dashing of Henry's entourage was William Marshal, the greatest knight of the period. Marshal would prove to be one of the most important figures in the Magna Carta story, and having served four kings loyally, his tales of heroism became the standard idea of what we imagine by chivalry. This was largely the case because his five sons later commissioned a book about him.

Although born in England and proclaimed in his biography as an English hero, Marshal was like all aristocrats a Norman by origin. His grandfather Gilbert Giffard, literally 'chubby cheeks,' had come over with the Conqueror in 1066, and been given land in Wiltshire and served as the royal master-marshal, an old military office that involved the day-to-day running of the court and looking after the king's horses. William's father John had been a major baron during the Anarchy and a callous villain straight from central casting, right down to the disfigured face that he'd acquired after a church he was besieging had burned down and its lead roof had fallen on him. John Marshal had changed sides when it suited him and in one battle defeated another dubious figure, Robert Fitzhubert, a Flemish mercenary who had previously burned eighty monks to death while trapped inside a church. Fitzhubert had tried to capture Marshal's fortress by stealth but was defeated and hanged.

When he was just five, young William was given over as a hostage by his father, and when King Stephen threatened to hang him in front of the castle walls John had replied 'I still have the hammer and the anvil with which to forge still more and better sons!' Stephen's military advisors had also suggested using young William as a human catapult, but this didn't budge Marshal either, who seems to have been quite a stern father figure overall. However, Stephen didn't have the heart to go through with it and let the boy go.

William was a younger son and so, like any penniless young Norman aristocrat, he had made his way into fighting. Under the tutelage of his uncle, Earl Patrick, he had become a dashing warrior first in the service of Queen Eleanor against rebellious southern French barons and, after Patrick had inevitably been killed, Henry the Young King.

Marshal's biography, which is told in verse, is obviously hugely flattering, and in a way that sounds odd to modern ears, claiming that 'his body was so well-fashioned that, even if he had been created by the sculptor's chisel, his limbs would not have been so handsome.' It also stated that he had 'fine feet and hands,' with brown hair, dark complexion and, more strangely, 'a crotch so large. . . . that no noble could be his peer.' This was probably a reference to the width of his hips and horse-riding ability, and not anything unseemly, but it sounds like a rather strange thing for children to boast about their dad.

William Marshal claimed he had captured five hundred knights in his tournament career, which he managed to do partly because he was able to grab the bridle of another knight's horse, and partly because he had an unusually thick skull that allowed him to take the endless beatings his life inevitably involved. On one occasion, Marshal had to have his helmet wrenched off him, on a day in which he received such a pummeling from sword and mace blows that his helmet was crushed down 'to his scalp.' As one historian comments: 'All in all, Marshal seems to have regarded it as a splendid day.'[7]

By 1179, William had risen to become a 'knight banneret,' which meant someone in service to a lord, but important enough to carry his own banner, and had become the young king's leading knight despite being accused of adultery with Henry's wife Marguerite, literally 'doing it to the queen' as it was recorded at the time. Henry seems to have stopped speaking to him, which appears unusually lenient.

Attitudes to cheating were contradictory, 'for according to the ethos of chivalry an act of infidelity was no disgrace.' It was okay to have an affair with another man's wife so long as 'he observed the manners of polite society and was prepared to fight and to die for the lady he professed to love,' which is admittedly quite an expectation.[8]

However, sometimes people reacted badly. One of William's contemporaries, Count Philip of Flanders, accused a knight called Walter of Fontaines of committing adultery with his wife Isabel of Vermandois. Without a trial, he had the man beaten with cudgels until he was almost dead, and then a gallows was erected above a foul-smelling latrine. Poor Walter was stripped, bound, and strung up by his feet, upside down, his head dangling into the cesspit. He died of suffocation. However, despite all this Philip didn't divorce his wife—although it's safe to say the honeymoon period was over by now.*

Henry's frustration grew worse, however, after the old king almost died of fever and the young man geared himself up to rule—only for his dad to annoyingly pull through, leaving Henry left with little to do. He made the king give him a second coronation, with the new Archbishop of Canterbury doing the honors, and at a banquet he demanded his father wait hand and foot on him. When the older man complained, 'No other king in Christendom has such a butler,' young Henry replied: 'It is only fitting that the son of a count should wait on the son of a king.' History does not record the angry middle-aged monarch's response.

Then, after a very public argument in 1173, Henry started an open rebellion, joined by powerful landowners such as the earls of Norfolk, Chester, Derby, and Leicester. The Revolt of 1173–74 ultimately was a very bad-tempered family argument that unwillingly involved the whole country but it also served as a precursor to the Barons' Wars against the king's son and grandson, John and Henry III.

The conflict was stirred up by Eleanor, who had now finished her days of giving birth—eight children in total—and was free to indulge in her main interest, scheming. Eleanor seems to have fallen out with her husband over his relentless adultery, in particular his favorite mistress Rosamund Pike— 'fair Rosamund, the rose of the world.' Rosamund died in 1176, in mysterious circumstances, which was a shame as Henry had at one point planned on marrying her to his youngest son.

---

*　Philip may have just made up the whole accusation so he could take his wife's family's land.

The young king also made a deal with William, king of the Scots, to give him Northumberland in return for his help against his father. This was quite reckless, especially as the Scots had invaded only twenty years earlier and caused mayhem in the north. The Caledonian king accepted, 'and the Scottish army "armed men and naked" poured across the border.'[9] However this invasion 'was of the usual kind, devoid of any strategic plan; the border castles were in turn besieged, though few were taken; the land was devastated and plundered; grim atrocities were perpetrated.' Then the Scots were all beaten, as was young Henry.

After the king had been reconciled with his heir, he demanded that his second and third sons, Richard and Geoffrey, do homage to their elder brother. Richard refused and, just sixteen, he persuaded his fifteen-year-old brother to join him in rebellion. If young Henry sounded like an awful man, then his unruly siblings were even worse. Geoffrey was described by chronicler Roger of Howden as 'that son of perdition, that son of iniquity,' while Gerald of Wales called him a smooth-tongued hypocrite 'overflowing with words, soft as oil, possessed, by his syrupy and persuasive eloquence, of the power of dissolving the apparently indissoluble, able to corrupt two kingdoms with his tongue; of tireless endeavor, a hypocrite in everything, a deceiver and a dissembler.' Not a fan, then. The nicest thing a modern historian could say of Geoffrey was that he was 'a worthless creature, who spent his life in aimless killing and plundering.'[10]

Richard, meanwhile, had spent much of his youth in Aquitaine with his mother, and was always much closer to her and her homeland than to his father, with whom he had a difficult relationship, to say the least.

In 1174, the two brothers took up arms against their father, encouraged in this weird Freudian rebellion by their mother, as well as the King of Scotland. However, Eleanor supposedly fled in men's clothing to France, where her ex-husband Louis VII handed her back to the king; she now spent the next fifteen years in prison at the behest of her husband.* Her boys were forced to submit, the feisty young homicidal maniac Richard begging for forgiveness; father and son made up.

Henry II must have wondered what he'd done to deserve all of this, aside from murdering the Archbishop of Canterbury and invading Ireland. Yet more trouble was to come: in the autumn of 1182, young Henry asked his father for Normandy and some other territory 'to support knights in his service.' He was twenty-seven and still had nothing to do with his life. The young king stormed off to Paris when his demands were rejected, but his father wooed him back with a raise in his allowance.

Eventually, Richard agreed to do homage to his older brother if his lordship over Aquitaine was recognized. However, the young king refused, as he was secretly in league with rebels there to overthrow him, the barons of the south being sick of Richard's cruelty. Henry now declared war on his father *and* brother, and Geoffrey was sent to arrange a conference with the rebels but then joined them, betraying his father for a second time.

However, in 1183, King Henry was distraught with grief when his eldest son died in the Dordogne. The young man became sick while plundering a shrine, succumbing while holding a ring his father had sent him as a token of forgiveness; the older Henry had refused his request to visit because he suspected a trap. In one of his last acts the young man had begged Marshal to take the cloak that he wore and go to Jerusalem on crusade.

The devastated king lamented: 'He cost me so much, but I wish he had lived to cost me more.' Such was the glamour attached to

---

* In her rebellion, Eleanor outraged many people by her unladylike behavior, her escape dressed as a man being symbolic of taking on male roles. She was told off by Archbishop of Rouen who quoted St. Paul 'unless you return to your husband you will be the cause of general ruin,' which turned out to be pretty true.

young Henry that after his death the people of Le Mans kidnapped the body on its way to Rouen because they wanted it for their local church.

Geoffrey was kicked to death by a horse during a tournament three years later, although there is no record of even his father mourning him. However, Philip the Dauphin of France is said to have been so distraught he jumped in the grave, screaming and wailing; whether or not this was genuine or for show from the scheming prince we can't know. Geoffrey left behind a wife, Constance of Brittany, who had been forcibly married to him so the Angevins could grab her country; she was two months pregnant.

But the king's woes were far from over. He angered his new heir Richard by his generosity to John, who had been born in 1166 as an afterthought and had therefore not been allocated any land, so earning his nickname 'Jean San Terre' or 'Lackland.' So, as well as having Ireland as his plaything, John's father gave him three castles in Normandy, which was nice, although this was still not as good as getting Brittany (Geoffrey), Aquitaine (Richard), or Normandy and England (Henry).

After Geoffrey's death, the king demanded that Richard hand over his own personal fiefdom of Aquitaine to his brother. Richard, although widely hated in the region for his violence, sadism, and rape, was not about to give up this rich source of revenue, which also had emotional significance as the home of Eleanor. Richard, who was close to his mother, perhaps weirdly so, now started a new uprising against the old man, with he and Eleanor joined by the new king of France.

In 1180, Philip, the Dauphin of France, had fallen sick, and in desperation his father King Louis traveled to Canterbury to pray with Henry at the shrine of Becket; this had the added advantage of slightly showing up the king of England for having, well, murdered him. Young Prince Philip recovered but unfortunately on the way back Louis died of a stroke, so the mission wasn't a total success.

Now Richard went into alliance with the new king, who wanted to expand his realm and was 'willing to break promises, betray friendships and wage bloody wars to achieve this goal.'[11] In fairness to Richard, he had repeatedly asked his father to ensure his inheritance and the old man had refused to, possibly because he was all along planning to stitch him up and give it instead to his favorite, John.

Full war broke out on the border of the Angevin and French kings' territories in 1189, with Marshal in charge of the scorched earth policy, the deliberate aim being to terrorize the inhabitants of enemy lands. This was quite common in medieval war, for as that wet liberal Count Philip of Flanders advised: 'Destroy your foes and lay waste their country, by fire and burning let all be set alight, that nothing be left for them, either in wood or meadow, of which in the morning they could have a meal.' It rather goes without saying that this wasn't much fun for civilians caught in the middle, who suffered far more than aristocratic soldiers. As the great medieval historian A. L. Poole said: 'For the higher ranks, war was, in part at least, a game governed by the strict code of chivalry; it was only the unfortunate peasantry and other non-combatants who suffered from the savage plundering of the routiers.'[12]

In May 1189, the two sides met at Le Mans, Henry's birthplace. Richard's demands included the marriage of Alice, the king of France's sister, confirmation of his succession, and that John accompany him on crusade, which the king had vetoed. It's not that Richard especially wanted John's help fighting, but that he suspected that if he went away John would conspire against him (totally accurately as it happened). With their armies behind them, father and son met here where they embraced, and to those in the distance it looked like they had made peace, in modern terms a touching 'I love you pa' scene from a schmaltzy Hollywood film—although what the old king actually whispered in his ear was 'God spare me long enough to take revenge on you' (alas, he didn't).

In the no-man's-land between negotiations, Richard was almost killed by William Marshal, who charged straight at the rebellious prince. Neither was wearing armor, and with the famous tournament champion bearing down at him, Richard shouted 'By God's legs do not kill me, Marshal, that would be wrong, I am unarmed.' At the last moment, William ran his lance into the prince's poor innocent horse instead, replying 'No, I will not kill you, I shall leave that to the devil.'[13] This is how his own biography records the incident; how likely it is that two men in the thick of such violence would have come up with crisp cinematic dialogue is up to you to believe. Marshal's biographic poem might have slightly massaged the truth a little bit.

At the time, a mural owned by the king was on display in Winchester Castle, which Gerald of Wales described as showing 'an eagle with four of its young perching on it, one on each wing with a third on its back, tearing the parent with beaks and talons, while a fourth just as big as the other stands on its neck, waiting for a chance to peck out its eyes.' The painting, Henry said, was about him: 'The eagle's four young are my sons, who won't stop tormenting me till I'm dead. The youngest of whom I'm so fond will hurt me more painfully and fatally than the rest put together.'

Indeed, at the last moment, and in secret, John had joined the rebels. At his camp, the ailing Henry asked to be told the list of men who had supported Richard. The vice chancellor opened it and said: 'Sire, so Jesus Christ help me, the first which is written down here is Lord John, your son.' When the king saw his favorite child's name he said 'You have said enough.' He surrendered to the king of France in July 1189 and two days later his head basically exploded with rage, the king dying of a huge brain hemorrhage, and 'a stream of clotted blood burst forth from his nose and mouth.'

Of all his sons, only one stood by him on his deathbed, his bastard Geoffrey Plantagenet, the product of the king's youthful dalliance with Ykenai, a 'base-born, common harlot who stooped

to all uncleanliness,' according to one—perhaps not entirely sympathetic—chronicler. Her son ended up becoming Archbishop of
York, which showed there was some social mobility, providing you
were prepared to have sex with the monarch. As the king had said to
the young man during a previous rebellion: 'You alone have proved
yourself my lawful and true son, the others are the real bastards.'

CHAPTER 6

The Lionheart
and the Crusades

As soon as King Henry died, his immediate household staff began looting the corpse, stealing 'his clothes, his jewels, his money as much as each of them could take' and this 'rabble' left the body of the king lying on a bed wearing only breaches and shorts. When Marshal, a few miles away, learned of the king's death he led a team to the remains, covering the body and remaining by its side; the knight stood vigil as his former master was taken to the abbey of Fontevraud waiting for the new king to arrive. But when Richard went to visit his father's corpse as it lay in state, it is said the old man's ears bled, as 'his spirit was angered by his approach,' traditionally the sign of a murderer being in a room. Richard had betrayed his father, and his even more awful brother in turn would betray him.

Richard Coeur de Lion, as he became known, was a ferocious warrior, and it's not clear whether the nickname 'Lionheart' was as complimentary as it sounds or a reference to his inhumanity, which was widely recognized, or a mixture of the two. Richard spent all of six months in England during a ten-year reign, the rest of which he was causing mayhem in the Middle East as head of the Crusades, or in France fighting his fellow crusaders in various off-season warm-up wars. By all accounts, he absolutely loved every minute of it, laughing his way through the slaughter right up to the point when a crossbow bolt fatally hit him. Richard was a fantastically good military leader and he also looked the part of a king, with dazzling blue eyes, long legs, a big chest, and golden-reddish hair. He was the greatest warrior of his age, partly because of his genius for the logistics of war, but mostly because he just loved violence; a monastic chronicler accused him of 'immoderate use of arms from his earliest youth,' and this continued for the rest of his days.

Although Henry II spent only a third of his reign in England, most of it in Normandy, while he preferred the Loire Valley most of all, Richard tried to avoid the place altogether if he could help it, complaining that 'England is cold and always raining.' At one point, he even tried to sell the entire country to the Holy Roman Emperor. Richard also managed to make enemies with almost everyone he met en route to the Holy Land, and this would cost England a king's ransom. Literally. Whatever the rights and wrongs of the holy war, they were very expensive, and the monarch's escapades bankrupted the country and in particular cost the barons dearly. These were among the causes of the rebellion of 1215.

Yet despite squandering all of England's money on a futile war in the Middle East, Richard's PR team still managed to leave him remembered as some great national hero. Bizarrely, Richard I is the only monarch with a statue next to Parliament, when he is just about the least deserving of all, with the possible exception of Hardicnut, the eleventh-century Viking who drank himself to death after only two years on the throne. They say that death and taxes are the only two inevitabilities in life, but under the Lionheart they both came sooner rather than later.

Richard's popularity had much to do with his straight dealing and lack of malice; although violent and brutal, he was not sly. One of his first acts was to forgive William Marshal, allowing him to marry Strongbow's daughter, Isabel de Clare, something Henry II had promised him—a lottery win if ever there was one, as she came with most of south Wales and eastern Ireland.

After he had arrived by the old king's corpse, Richard asked Marshal to come with him to the countryside. After a pause the new king said, 'Marshal, the other day you intended to kill me, and you would have, without a doubt, if I hadn't deflected your lance with my arm.' The knight replied that it was not his intention to kill him, and he could have if he wanted to. He might well have expected the king to have him executed or exiled, but instead Richard 'in effect, made William a millionaire overnight.'[1]

Richard sent Marshal to England to 'take charge of my land and all my other interests,' with a secret message for his mother in jail, although frustratingly his biography doesn't say what it was. The new king forgave all those who had stayed loyal to his father, and made peace with Philip of France, paying him off with 40,000 silver marks for the return of Angevin land.

Finally after fifteen years of being a prisoner of her husband, Eleanor was freed and became de facto ruler of England. In another act of largesse, the new monarch released most of the people languishing in Henry's jails, because Eleanor 'had learned by experience that confinement is distasteful to mankind, and that it is a most delightful refreshment to the spirits to be set free therefrom.' Rather predictably, there followed an explosion in crime, but it also made Richard popular because many were in prison for having broken the detested forest laws. Introduced by William the Conqueror to protect the vast royal hunting grounds—one-third of the entire country—these included such punishments as blinding for anyone who captured a hare, which even by the low standards of the twelfth century was considered draconian.

Richard then turned up in England with Stephen of Tours—the old king's least popular minister—in chains. All of this sort of stuff was tremendously popular with the gormless peasants who constituted most of the population.[2]

For his coronation in September 1189, and to show that he was God's chosen one, Richard made the Archbishop of Canterbury anoint him with holy oil on the chest, hands, and head—a tradition that pretty much survives today, although Queen Victoria removed the chest part, as by that stage English people had grown a bit uncomfortable with that sort of thing. Richard's coronation was absurdly elaborate, attended by churchmen in purple silk, with candles and incense, the king being escorted along streets covered in cloth, with singers behind him, followed by the great and good of the realm. After this, Archbishop Baldwin anointed him with a tiny silver spoon, and he was then crowned and given a scepter and golden rod.

Following his coronation, Richard held an enormous party, with 1,770 pitchers of ale, 900 cups, and 5,050 dishes, a scene that one imagines must have involved lots of Robin Hood–style japes and general medieval cheer; unless you were Jewish of course. Richard, not really getting into the whole interfaith spirit of things, commanded that the 'enemies of Christ' weren't to be allowed in. When some rabbis tried to bring gifts for the king, a riot ensued, the start of a sinister new trend across Europe; however, Richard punished the rioters with extreme violence, out of 'greed rather than compassion—he wanted to fleece the entire [Jewish] community to pay for his crusade.'[3]

Richard's long-held ambition was to follow in the footsteps of his great-grandfather Fulk by leading a holy war, and the whole king of England thing was something of a distraction. So the following Tuesday after his coronation, Richard, in effect, sold the entire country, with royal estates and offices going in a sale, the king flogging every job that could be flogged. The chancellorship, a position that entailed running the country while the king was away, went to a Norman, William Longchamp, who paid £3,000 for the honor. Even people who already held positions had to stump up more or the king would sell them to someone else. Richard joked: 'I would have sold London could I have found a buyer.' He also sold his rights to Scotland for 10,000 marks, its king William of Scotland having previously been forced to sign a humiliating peace treaty with Henry II after his last invasion that had seen him dragged around England and France in chains for months.

The Crusades were a sort of gap year of the time, except instead of building a well or teaching school kids in Africa, you got to kill some Arabs; that's if you didn't die in agony from dysentery or get beheaded by some bearded maniac.

The Third Crusade came about after the Christian Kingdom of Jerusalem had been reconquered by the Muslims in 1187, news of which had caused Pope Urban III to die of shock. The rulers of England, France, and Germany pledged their support, and to encourage recruits, emperors and kings promised rich rewards on Earth; while the Pope said anyone who died on Crusade would enter Heaven in a state of grace, with a soul unstained by any previous wrongdoing. There were other pressures, of course—men who didn't take up the cross were given distaff and wool in the street, the equivalent of handing them a white feather in the First World War or perhaps shouting 'paedo' at them today.*

Henry II had promised to take up the cross but had never really had any intention of doing so, even though he was related to Baldwin IV, the unfortunate leper king of Jerusalem. There had also been talk of John going on crusade or even becoming ruler of the Holy Land, an offer informally made to him in 1185 but which his father had wisely vetoed.

Many crusaders were extremely heroic. James of Avesnes fell at Arsuf after being isolated from his comrades and killing fifteen

---

* Marshal didn't take the cross because as his biography stated he 'had already made the journey to the Holy Land to seek God's mercy . . . whatever anyone else might tell you, that is how matters were arranged.' So, that clears that up.

Muslims before his death, and his corpse was later found surrounded by dead infidels. But much of the time, they were fanatical and moronic in the extreme, and often—out of sheer dimness or otherwise—they attacked other Christians, who they were supposed to be helping. The enterprise would reach its nadir in 1204 when the crusaders sacked Constantinople, the leading Christian city in the world, a blow from which it never recovered.

The logistics involved were immense. Richard I had sixty thousand horseshoes made before setting off, as well as turning fourteen thousand pigs into cured ham. Soon, an appropriate omen went his way when reconstruction work at Glastonbury Abbey led to the discovery of two bodies, which just happened to be those of Arthur and Guinevere, the sixth-century, nonexistent king and queen of Britain—which was incredibly good luck. Glastonbury Abbey had burned down in 1184 and the monks there were in desperate need of money to finance a new building, so they might not have been entirely honest when they made this miraculous discovery, as there were clear financial incentives toward being associated with the mythical King Arthur. As anyone who has been to Glastonbury today, with its plethora of 'magik' shops, can attest to, this is still a big selling point.

Alongside Arthur and Guinevere was a sword, which Richard assumed to be Excalibur and took with him; he then swapped it with the dim-witted king of Sicily for four ships and fifteen galleys. Such deals were quite common. Hoping to conquer Hungary, one German emperor exchanged a chunk of Switzerland for a piece of the 'True Cross,' of which there was said to be enough bits going around to construct a medium-sized boat. Still, when the war came about, his successor did beat Hungary, so who are we to say it wasn't a wise transaction.

Long before he even reached the Levant, Richard managed to get into trouble. His army first landed in Sicily, which was ruled by King Tancred, a dwarfish man, rather cruelly said to resemble a monkey with a crown placed on its head. Although Tancred was from Sicily's Norman ruling class, the people of the island were largely Greek Orthodox, who lived alongside Jews and Muslim Arabs in relative harmony by the standards of the day. The Normans had first arrived on the island in the eleventh century as tourists on their way back from Palestine but ended up conquering it, as they tended to do; but they were fairly tolerant as rulers.

Then several thousand highly armed, drunk crusaders rowed into view. There were already tensions: Tancred was the bastard cousin of the previous king, William II, who had been married to Richard's sister Joan, and the new ruler had refused to allow her back or to return her dowry, so he had already gotten off to a bad start with the Lionheart.

Alongside Richard for the jaunt was Philip II of France, his ally, rival, and enemy, who had grown from being a weedy adolescent into a devious adult. Under the previous reign, Richard and Philip became close: 'Between the two of them, there grew up so great an affection that King Henry was much alarmed.'[4] However, it did not last long. Philip was described by one contemporary as 'one-eyed, red-faced, unkempt, charmless, a timid young man fearful of assassins and hard-mouthed horses.' It was Philip who built medieval Paris, and he planned to expand the size of his kingdom, at the expense of the Angevins. When he was born, citizens of the French capital had rung bells and lit bonfires, declaring 'by the grace of God there is born to us this night a king who shall be a hammer to the king of the English.' Despite Philip's cunning schemes however, in a predictable, cartoonish way the Lionheart always beat him in battle.

Richard and Philip had to arrange to leave at the same time, as neither trusted the other not to attack while he was away, even though the Pope had ruled against it.

In Sicily, Richard and Philip got into an argument with Tancred, who was alarmed at the sight of this traveling army turning up on his island, and a fight soon broke out between the locals and tourists. With two groups of men sharing the same space, and with alcohol involved, the argument could have started over anything, although the chronicler Ambroise said at the time that the crusaders were 'anxious to make friends with the women of Sicily,' which is never going to go down too well.

The situation got out of control and Richard ended up sacking the city of Messina—and this was supposed to just be an overnight stay as guests.*

It illustrated his incredible fighting skills: he took Messina quicker than it would take for a priest to say Mass, so Ambroise said. But his diplomatic talents weren't quite of the same quality. After Richard conquered the town he began building a castle, which he sensitively called 'Castle Kill the Greeks.' To everyone's horror, Richard then decided they would winter in Sicily, and to make matters worse for the poor Sicilians, it was reported that the German Emperor and his army were now on their way.

Richard then fell out with Philip, and the cause was a woman, or Richard's lack of interest in one. In recent years, there has been a fashion for suggesting that Richard was gay, a case first made in 1947, but there's no real evidence, and certainly no one mentioned it at the time. The main argument seems to be that he was very close to his mother, as well as his wet nurse, Hodierna, who is (as far as anyone knows) the only wet nurse to have a parish named after her, Knoyle Hodierne in Wiltshire.† Another supposed pointer is that Philip and Richard regularly shared a bed when they were allies against Henry, although medieval historians say

---

*   Before arriving in Sicily, Richard had also caused a brawl in Calabria, the 'toe' of Italy, when he saw a falcon in a village and insisted on taking it with him.

†   Hodierna's son Alexander Neckam, born on the same night as the Lionheart, became the first European to study magnetism.

there is no sexual significance to this and that men would regularly bunk together. And on another occasion a hermit rebuked Richard for his sins, shouting 'Remember the destruction of Sodom.' At the time, though, that would have referred to any extramarital sex.* However the best evidence that Richard wasn't gay was that he is known to have committed multiple rapes as ruler of Aquitaine; so desperately insecure men who want him as a role model can rest assured. He also sired at least one bastard, which is admittedly tame by his father's standards. More likely, he was just more interested in fighting than anything else, and as one modern historian suggests, Richard's 'tastes did not lie in the direction of marriage.'

In Sicily, he argued with Philip over the latter's sister, Alice, who Richard had been engaged to for twenty years. Alice had, at the age of eight, been sent to England to marry but had been kept waiting by Henry II for political reasons, effectively a prisoner her whole life. To make matters worse, Henry had supposedly had sexual relations with her. Richard rather offended the French king by saying that Alice's morals were too questionable for marriage, which could have been more tactfully put, but she was rumored to have had a child by Richard's father, so we can see his reluctance; it would have been slightly on the weird side.

Philip and Richard also fell out over flags, a subject that seems somewhat childish eight centuries later but was hugely important.

---

* When Richard became ill, he began to believe the hermit was right, although the Lionheart swallowed any old rubbish that hermits told him. Joachim of Fiore, the wild hermit of Calabria, predicted that a third age was nigh, and the Muslim leader Saladin was the sixth of the seven great enemies of the Church, the last being the antichrist, who would get the job of Pope before revealing himself. Richard, who didn't like Pope Clement III, thought it all made sense and waited in vain for the pontiff to eventually reveal his true identity.

Philip was furious that Richard had flown his flag over Messina and demanded that his also be erected.

As if things weren't bad enough, Eleanor of Aquitaine then arrived in town with Berengaria, a Spanish princess she intended her son to marry; despite being seventy, Richard's mother had ridden all the way to Madrid to find a wife for her boy. Either she was a calculating politician or one of those mothers totally deluded about her son's sexual orientation. Though they did eventually marry, Berengaria became the only English queen to never visit England, and she and Richard never had sex.[5] Apart from that, the marriage went splendidly.

Luckily, Richard escaped the island just as his mother arrived, long after Philip, outraged, had sailed ahead to Palestine.

At this point, the Templars, the famous medieval religious-military-banking group founded in 1119 to defend pilgrims in the Holy Land, turn up in the story. Having fled Sicily, Philip had been captured by Isaac, the tyrant of Cyprus, and Richard, in what he later described as a 'fit of pique,' invaded it (again, a Christian country), freed the king of France, and conquered the island; he then sold it to the Templars. Despite their monastic origins, the Templars had grown incredibly rich through patronage and support across western Christendom and sort of ended up inventing banking, as they were able to transfer large amounts of money across Europe and the Middle East. In fact, this wealth would be their undoing when the Crusades all started going wrong, and they were destroyed by Philip IV of France in 1312, although they continue to exist in the minds of conspiracy-theory-loving imbeciles.

The tyrant of Cyprus was a strange one; he had bluffed his way into the job, having arrived on the island with forged documents supposedly from the ruler of Constantinople stating that he was the new governor, and by the time anyone found out about the forgery, he had installed himself as dictator. He had incurred Richard's ire by taking the remains of a crusader shipwreck, which under convention he was entitled to, but was not the sort of thing you did with Richard.

Isaac surrendered to the English king on the condition that he was not 'clapped in iron,' and the Lionheart agreed—and had special silver chains made for him. Richard then, in an act of petty spite, made the Greeks shave off their beards to conform with western ways.*

It was already turning out to be some trip. But what with the battles, the risk of some disgusting disease, and the dangers of long-distance travel, the Crusades were hugely risky adventures. In 1191, at Acre, Richard and Philip both got trench mouth, an infection every bit as horrible as it sounds, which caused their nails and hair to fall out. The holy war was relentlessly grim most of the time, and in the winter of 1190 some two hundred crusaders a day were dying of illness and starvation.

But there were plus points for the lads on tour if you were interested in violence and the ladies. At Acre, the local women cosied up to the Crusader men; that is, people think that's what the Arab Imad ad-Din was getting at when he said 'They made themselves targets for men's darts, offered themselves to the lance's blows, made javelins rise towards shields. . . . They interwove leg with leg, caught lizard after lizard in their holes, guided pens to inkwells, torrents to the valley bottom, swords to scabbards, firewood to stoves.' Had Imad been born in a different time and place, he could have made quite a living writing erotic fiction.

They also got to play around with some fairly awesome weaponry, with European military technology starting to advance at the time, in

---

*   To pass the time, Richard and one of his knights, William des Barres, had a joust. When Richard was unable to unhorse his opponent, he became so angry that he 'uttered threats against him' and banished des Barres, and the whole thing turned into an unseemly brawl.

particular big siege weapons; Philip had enormous trebuchets built, two with the excessively macho names God's Own Sling and The Wicked Neighbor, capable of firing 350 pounds of material at the enemy.

Philip, however, was almost continually ill in the Holy Land since arriving, and he really didn't like the ordeal at all. Richard seemed to love it: when he arrived in the Middle East, he just assumed command and no one questioned it, even when he got sick. Even then, 'he pursued hostilities with far more vigor from his sickbed than Philip Augustus had ever done in full health.'[6]

Their comrade at arms, the German legend Frederick Barbarossa, had had an even worse war. Barbarossa was famed for having led his people on crusade against the pagans of northeast Europe with his Teutonic Knights. He was so good at siege terror tactics that his troops were known for playing football with their enemies' severed heads 'and [to] torture captured defenders by scalping them or cutting off their hands and feet, to provide amusement and relief from the boredom that naturally accompanied such an attritional method of warfare.'[7]

However, the most famous warrior in Christendom had barely arrived in the Middle East before drowning in a mundane accident, leaving many of the Germans to give up.

In October 1191, at Jaffa, Richard almost got caught when some Turks ambushed his party. One of his knights, William de Preaux, pretended to be the king, giving him time to escape as he fought off the infidels; the Turks greatly admired de Preaux for this and took him alive; Richard's last act before returning home would be to pay his ransom.

But though the fate of the holiest of cities was at stake, throughout these campaigns Richard and Philip were constantly bickering, even quarreling via messengers while both were seriously ill.

Richard had by now also fallen out with Duke Leopold of Austria, over the issue of flags once again; the flags issue was important not just for the sake of ego but because raising the flag meant the troops from that country were free to loot. This time it happened after the fall of Acre, on July 12, 1191, when Leopold put his standard up to try to bask in the glory, and Richard's soldiers tore it down. The Austrian swore his revenge.

The following month came the most controversial episode of the Crusades when Richard broke a treaty and ordered the execution of 2,500 Muslim prisoners: 'Some were hanged, others were killed by the sword, while the Muslim cavalry attacked in a frenzy of anger, trying to break through to the scene of the execution; but they failed.'[8] The reason Richard did this was because his opponent Saladin would not return to him a bit of the 'True Cross' that Jesus died on, which in retrospect doesn't seem like very good justification. Although there was a military reason for this massacre—Richard couldn't bring with him all these prisoners as he marched on Jerusalem—we can't be entirely certain that Jesus would approve.

Philip had meanwhile left the Holy Land on July 22, saying he was too ill to continue; some of his men chose to stay with Richard, which was yet another humiliation. And when Philip returned home, he was soon 'imprudently boasting that he was going to devastate the lands of the king of England.'

And after Acre was conquered, the Pisans and Genoese, who hated each other more than they hated any Muslims, plunged the crusaders into an absurd civil war.

CHAPTER SEVEN

A King's Ransom

Perhaps the worst thing about the king's addiction to overseas adventures was that it meant his younger brother John was left in charge. Upon his father's death, John had been made Count of Mortain in Normandy, and had been given numerous castles and estates in England and France, as well as all the revenues of Somerset, Dorset, Devon, Cornwall, Derbyshire, and Nottinghamshire. He now personally owned Ireland, the southwest of England, Lancashire, and southwestern Normandy, but he also wanted to be king. When Richard departed for Palestine, he had made specific instructions that John was not to enter England for three years while he was away, but he was persuaded to let him stay by their mother. So from 1190, once Richard headed off, John was basically an irresponsible twenty-something in his own country-sized Playboy mansion. When warned that his brother would probably try to seize the throne while he was away on crusade, Richard replied: 'my brother John is not the man to conquer a country if there is anyone to offer the feeblest resistance.' Which turned out to be fairly accurate.

It was not long before Lackland was conspiring against his brother, and against the chancellor Longchamp, spreading the idea that because he was foreign he didn't really understand English ways and should be ignored.

The Norman chancellor was not very popular, to put it mildly; he made enemies with many of the most powerful men, including William Marshal and Bishop Godfrey of Winchester—who, thanks to Longchamp, was forced to give up his lands and castles despite having paid the king £3,000 for them only a year before. Longchamp had numerous faults, among them 'over-confidence, inordinate love of power, aggrandizement of his family, lack of tact, and a complete failure to understand the English whom he openly professed to despise.' Both clergy and laity found him to be 'an intolerable tyrant.'[1] It didn't help that Longchamp introduced the French style of being served food by a kneeling servant, and that he couldn't even speak English, nor to mention that he traveled around with an entourage of one thousand men.[2]

Longchanp was also physically unfortunate, a 'short, ugly, deformed figure,'[3] and Gerald of Wales likened him to an ape. As one historian put it: 'If his enemies are to be believed, Bishop Longchamp looked like a cross between Shakespeare's Richard III and Tolkien's Gollum.'[4]

Not that there were any goodies in this particular drama. John's chief ally in his scheming was Bishop Hugh Nunant of Coventry, who was said to be so sinful that after his deathbed confession no one could be found who was willing to absolve him.

Richard had sent the Archbishop of Canterbury, Baldwin, to the holy land ahead of him. Baldwin was a controversial figure who as one chronicler put it, 'was more damaging to Christianity than Saladin.' When the churchman arrived in 1190, he got bogged down in a succession dispute after the Queen of Jerusalem had died, and was in the process of excommunicating everyone when he succumbed himself soon after.

In 1191, news reached England about Archbishop Baldwin's demise and Longchamp, who was also the pope's legate in England, was therefore effectively in charge of the Church. He soon imprisoned Geoffrey Plantagenet, the Archbishop of York, who was also the king's half-brother, and ignored a royal command sent from the king in the Middle East.

The various bishops and archbishops were constantly at one another's throats. Geoffrey Plantagenet had been made archbishop under Richard even though there were complaints from the locals, namely that he wasn't even a priest. Geoffrey swaggered around, and once drunkenly put a golden cup cover on his head and said 'Would not a crown look well on this head?' This during a period when paranoid, dictatorial monarchs were in charge was tantamount to screaming 'please behead me.' Once installed, he claimed that any grants made by the king in his province would need his consent; Richard had brought him down to earth by stripping him of his land.

John, for perhaps the only time in his life, was now the hero of the hour, ordering Longchamp to leave the kingdom, and after a brief struggle, the bishop fled the country in 1191 disguised as a prostitute, escaping despite a sex-starved fisherman trying to assault him en route.

By the winter of 1191–92 John was in military control of London and began to conspire with King Philip, but any talk of open rebellion was halted in February when his mother heard about it, crossed over to England, and held meetings of the Great Council, making her son back down. Having put him in his place, she then went about sorting out the Church, forcing the warring northern bishops to make up (Archbishop Geoffrey of York had excommunicated the Bishop of Durham at the time). John's unrest was triggered by the treaty between Richard and Tancred of Sicily, which named Richard's nephew Arthur of Brittany as his heir; this was done so that Arthur could be more valuable when he was married off to Tancred's daughter. Meanwhile, news of Richard's marriage to Berengia in the spring now also threatened John further; if they produced an heir that is, which would entail touching each other.

Having signed a treaty with Saladin in September 1192, Richard now had to return home, and to avoid France en route in case Philip's men got him; however, he had also fallen out with the Austrian ruler, Leopold, so that whole swathe of central Europe was a no-no, too. But on the way, the king was shipwrecked. He landed, of all places, in Austrian territory. Despite disguising himself as a lumberjack, or possibly a monk, his expensive gloves gave him away, and Leopold's men found him in a 'house of ill repute' (which could mean either a brothel or poor man's home). Leopold sold him as a hostage to the German emperor, Heinrich VI, who in turn demanded a ransom from the English Crown.

Medieval contracts could be as complex as any Hollywood deal. The agreement between Heinrich and the English included 100,000 marks as payment but also stipulated that Richard's niece was to marry Leopold's son; that Isaac of Cyprus was to be released by Richard's men; that Richard would have to bring fifty galleys and two hundred knights to Heinrich's invasion of Sicily; and that Heinrich would have to give Leopold two hundred hostages. Meanwhile, when Richard was captured, John announced that his brother was dead and began open rebellion against him, rushing to Paris in January 1193 to do homage to Philip.

King Philip had planned to invade Normandy while Richard was still in Palestine, but none of his neighbors would go to war against a crusader, as the Pope had strictly forbidden such a thing. But he found a coconspirator in John, who betrayed both God and his own brother in one act. Even French chroniclers who disliked Richard, such as Philip's biographer Rigord de Saint-Denis, were scandalized that the younger brother would do such a thing. But then it was a sort of family tradition that went right back to old Fulk the Black. Now Lackland gave up large parts of Normandy to the French as part of his deal, so much so that Philip 'thought him a fool' and was shocked by his lack of sense.

It is not like Richard had not been warned about his brother. On April 5, 1192, he had received a letter from Longchamp about an attempted coup by John but he continued fighting, and in May he launched a new military offensive. At the end of the month, he got a second letter saying John was conspiring with Philip; instead Richard made another attempt at capturing Jerusalem.

John and Philip struggled to find allies to help them. King William of Scotland refused to join in because Richard had freed him and to fight him would be dishonorable; likewise, Richard's allies, including Dietrich, Count of Holland, Henry, Duke of Brabant and the unlikely named Archbishop Adolf of Cologne, all remained loyal. He had that effect on people, while Philip and John didn't. It's telling that despite the cost of the King's ransom, there seems to have been little appetite for the alternative, John; people were prepared to pay four year's annual revenue to keep him from power.

Their other devious plan was to get the Danish king, Canute VI, to invade; after all, no one had really heard from the Vikings for a while, but they were always up for a fight. However, as it turned out, the days of the Danes being a threat to anyone were long gone, and they were already well on their way to becoming the tediously reasonable peace lovers of today. Canute's invasion failed to materialize, and even if he'd succeeded he'd probably have just set up a center-Left coalition government anyway.

Philip and John also attempted to pay the emperor to keep Richard in prison for an extra year. Meanwhile, Richard's mum tried to intervene by writing to the Pope, signing her letter 'Eleanor by the wrath of God,' but it made no difference—the realm of England was forced to pay thirty-four tons of gold, four years' worth of government expenditure.[5]

The job of collecting this vast amount of cash fell on the chancellor and his sheriffs, and the king's ransom was soon followed by 'Saladin's Tithe,' a tax on all revenue in the kingdom to pay for the capture of Jerusalem. There was a certain amount of compulsion; while the negotiations were going on, Richard sent a letter to his mother asking that she note who contributed money so he might show his great thanks. In other words, anyone who didn't contribute would be noted. However, despite the huge cost involved, the Germans accompanying Richard's return were apparently so amazed by London's opulence they thought they could have gotten more for him.

This was onerous for the people back in England but for Richard, meanwhile, imprisonment was like jail for Mafia dons or Wall Street crooks in the 1970s. 'He was allowed to hold his court at Spires or Worms or wherever he might be, and to transact the business of his kingdom; his friends, who visited him in great numbers, were permitted to come and go unmolested; and he had his hawks sent to him to provide him with amusement.'[6]

During his confinement, Richard passed the time by playing practical jokes on his jailors, while a legend grew that the Lionheart's minstrel, Blondel de Nesle, looked for him by going around Germany singing his favorite tune until, finally, he responded from his cell. He also apparently wrote the love song *Ja nus hons pris* 'No man who is in prison,' which can still be found on an album called *Music of the Crusades*. Most likely, none of these stories are true.

Another legend put around to impress the gormless yokels at home has Richard's jailors setting a hungry lion on him, only for the jailor's daughter to fall in love with him and give him forty silk handkerchiefs with which to defend himself. Just what you need when fighting a lion, one would think, but at this point Richard calmly wraps the handkerchiefs around his hand, puts his arm down the animal's throat, and rips the beast's heart out and eats its still-beating organ—after first sprinkling salt on it—in front of the amazed Austrians. I think we can safely assume that story was unlikely to be true, as well, but the fact that these highly improbable tales attached themselves to the king suggests that some people were at least prepared to believe them. He was heroic. No one would believe such a story if it was John involved; women tended to go out of their way to avoid Richard's brother and if a similar tale had been made about him it would probably involve him pushing the jailer's daughter in front of the lion to save his own skin.

Richard finally made it back home in March 1194, Philip having sent a message to John: 'Look to yourself; the devil is loosed.' Although Lackland had fled to Normandy, his brother caught up with him at Lisieux, where he was surprisingly forgiving, telling him: 'Think no more of it, brother: you are but a child who has had evil counselors.' John was twenty-seven at the time. He showed repentance by inviting members of a French garrison at Evereux (his own side) to dinner where he had them murdered and their heads stuck on poles. John's lands were restored, and all was well that ended well (apart for the French soldiers, obviously). Richard stormed nearby Vernueuil, which had been besieged by King Philip, and there he supposedly kissed every member of the garrison defending it—but in a manly way, obviously.

On his return, the Lionheart besieged Nottingham, one of the very few areas that had sided with John in his woefully incompetent rebellion. At first, its defenders refused to give in, then he ordered gibbets to be raised and hanged a few captives in full view of everyone, which got the message across. According to Marshal's biography, the other soldiers were spared because of 'compassionate' king Richard who was 'so gentle and full of mercy.' Other sources say at least one of them was flayed alive and the others were starved to death in a dungeon—so compassionate perhaps for the standards of the twelfth century. However, such was the king's reputation that he didn't actually have to kill all his enemies; the governor of St. Michael's Mount in Cornwall died of fright on hearing of Richard landing in England.

As it was, Duke Leopold never received the money from the emperor, and on New Year's Eve 1194, he died of gangrene after crushing his foot in a riding accident. On his release, Isaac the

Tyrant went back to his old ways and made an audacious bid to seize Constantinople and become emperor, but he was poisoned. The Templars found Cyprus too much effort and ended up selling it on, for 40,000 Byzantine bezants, less than half as much as they'd paid for it. And they defaulted on the rest of the payment to Richard. As with all Middle East adventures, nothing ever goes to plan.

In the end, Richard's escapades had achieved very little, with Jerusalem still in Muslim hands, the king having never gotten closer than twelve miles away from it, although for centuries mothers in Turkey would warn their children of *Malik Rik*, King Richard, a bogeyman figure. However, historians are grateful for the Lionheart's adventures. Hubert Walter, who Richard made Chief Justiciar during his absence, thought it wise to record everything in case the king accused him of fiddling with the books, and government affairs have been written down ever since.

As a result, the day Richard's reign started became set as the date on which anyone who could establish they owned land on that day could confirm it was theirs by right, since often disputes about ownership went deep into the past to a time when no one could remember. So July 6, 1189, is officially the start of legal memory, or 'time immemorial.'

Walter is considered one of the best administrators the country ever had, responsible for creating a system of government we all depend on, but no one remembers him; only the man who ran around the Middle East arguing over flags.

CHAPTER EIGHT

Stealing from the Rich

A t the heart of the conflict that led to Magna Carta was money, and the Crown's relentless thirst for more of it. Around half of its clauses relate to financial disputes, and this had as much to do with Henry II and Richard I as it did with John.

The royals were not exactly the villains of the piece either; no doubt some barons missed the good old days of the Anarchy when local aristos could just do whatever they liked in their neighborhood. Others recognized the need for taxation but wanted it carried out more fairly.

There were other wider economic problems; the late twelfth century saw a big increase in inflation, partly because huge amounts of silver had been discovered in Switzerland in the 1160s. (And as with the dollar today, sterling was so respected that fake sterling mints were all over western Europe.) This inflation also encouraged people to keep records in order to stop getting ripped off.

Richard openly extorted money from nobles, one way being through forcing them to pay a fee to inherit their father's land, the 'reliefs' that were mentioned in Henry I's charter. This was the custom but the royals often charged absurd amounts, and then changed their minds when it wasn't enough. In 1193, one Staffordshire landowner agreed to pay 200 marks to succeed to his family estate; but the following year it was increased to 300.[1] Roger Bigod, the earl of Norfolk, was forced to pay 100 marks to protect his family against arbitrary seizure of his land. Then, for no reason whatsoever, the figure was increased to 700 marks. It was a shakedown on a massive scale.

The king's sheriffs were particularly very unpopular because they raised money for the Crown, but also took a cut, and so they had an incentive to squeeze as much out as possible. It is not surprising then that when the Robin Hood legend emerged, a sheriff should be cast as the villain, but who exactly the myth was based on is hard to tell. John had appointed one Ralph FitzStephen as forester of Sherwood, a position that allowed him to seize anything illegal within the forest, while another man, Sheriff of Nottingham Philip Marc, is named in Magna Carta as one of the foreign villains the barons want expelled, so he probably wasn't popular either. Other possible inspirations include Brian de Lisle, chief forester of Nottinghamshire and Derbyshire, chief justice of the forest in the early 1220s, and sheriff of Yorkshire in the 1230s; and Reginald De Grey, the sheriff of Nottinghamshire, who was pursuing rebels against Henry III's government in 1266–7.

The very first 'Robert Hod' (as he was identified) is mentioned in June 1225 in York, and by the 1260s it had become a sort of nom de plume for rural ne'er-do-wells. The Robin Hood legend was first written down by William Langland in the 1370s, but it was certainly around in the thirteenth century. If there was anyone who it was even loosely based on, he would have probably been active toward the end of Henry III's reign in the 1260s; this was the period after the Second Barons' War when the country was in a state of lawlessness. Among the outlaws of this period was Adam Gurdon, a Hampshire man who, according to an improbable legend, was tracked down by the future Edward I, who took him on in single combat and was so impressed by his courage he spared his life.[2] The first Robin Hood stories refer to 'King Edward,' and tradition linking the outlaw to John when the Lionheart was away on crusade only dates from the sixteenth century, and was widely popularized by Walter Scott in the nineteenth. (In fact, Nottingham, or Snottingham as it was originally called—after a Mr Snot, which means wise in Old English—was the most pro-John city during his rebellion against Richard.)

There may well have been a Robin of Loxley or Robert of Huntingdon, a dispossessed earl who had fallen foul of forestry officials, fighting against the Crown following Henry III's seizure of lands. But he probably wasn't very nice and most likely focused mainly on taking from the rich rather than redistributing it. And Robin Hood in the original story didn't prance around in green tights, but is portrayed as a maniac who hacks off an enemy's head at one point. It was only in the Victorian era, during a period of romanticism about the medieval period and rural life (popular among people who were safely far away from its ghastly reality) that Robin Hood as romantic outlaw really took hold; at the time, the story was popular among a certain type of yeoman who glorified stories about one of their own terrorizing the authorities, but most people viewed outlaws in basically the same way we would see a mugger hanging around your local park.

Partly the reason was that crime during this period was, by modern standards, absurdly high, with London having an annual murder rate between thirty-six and fifty-two per one hundred thousand compared to Britain's current national level of one in one hundred thousand.[1] Fourteenth century Oxford had an annual homicide rate of one hundred per one hundred thousand people, which is roughly twice the current level for Baltimore or Detroit.[4] For all the romantic notions that medieval villagers had a sense of community by living near to family and friends, the rates at which they murdered one another suggest that they weren't too pleased about it.

Because of logistics and the lack of crime detection, wrongdoers were rarely brought to justice. To take one example, in Northumberland in 1279, there were forty-three accidental deaths and seventy-two murders in a region that probably had only a few thousand people; just three of the murderers were caught, one was imprisoned, one was fined, one got out of it by pleading Benefit of Clergy, and the rest escaped, presumably to become outlaws.

Coroners' rolls are full of tales of horrific roadside crimes, including beatings, muggings, rapes, and murders by outlaws, none of whom had the slightest intention of giving to the poor. Travelers could expect to be attacked with knives, arrows, poleaxes, or any instrument sharp or blunt enough to cause injury. One unfortunate was dragged to a churchyard and had his toes cut off. Another, Nicholas Cheddleton from Marston, Staffordshire, was 'going along the King's highway with linen and cloth and other goods,' when he was ambushed by a group of thieves intent on murdering him. Cheddleton struck one over the head with a staff and killed him. He was found not guilty.

The political message of Robin Hood came much later, and in the Victorian period he became a figure of English resistance against French Norman rule, before evolving into an antiglobalization pseudo-commie and most recently a sort of disillusioned Iraq war veteran.

However, there were certainly movements suggesting discontent and figures during the twelfth century who did fight against the rich; at one point, London's poor and disillusioned, of which there were many, were moved to agitation by one 'William long beard,' a charismatic speaker who 'plotted great wickedness in the name of justice, a conspiracy of the poor against the rich. With his fiery eloquence, he inflamed both the poor and the moderately well-off with a desire for limitless freedom and happiness and with a hatred for the arrogance of the rich and noble which he painted in the blackest colors. At public meetings, he proclaimed himself the king of the poor, and their savior,' and also called himself the 'advocate of the people'; at St. Paul's he argued that the rich should bear the burden of financing the Crusade. In those days, of course, the authorities rather looked down on this sort of agitation, and it ended badly for the humble soldier—who was, in reality, a university-educated Anglo-Norman with the embarrassingly aristocratic name William Fitz Osbert, but who chose to play down his origins and instead grew his hair and beard long in tribute to his Saxon ancestry.[5]

In 1196, Fitz Osbert and his nine associates took sanctuary at St. Mary-le-Bow in the city but had to flee after the authorities set fire to the church.* It's a sign of how brutal these times were that the man who did this was the Archbishop of Canterbury. Fitz Osbert killed an officer who tried to arrest him but was caught. Afterwards he was bound to horses' tails and ripped to pieces, then dragged to Tyburn, west of London, where he and his men were hanged in chains.† He claimed to have a following of fifty-two thousand supporters ready to back him with an uprising, but that figure turned out to be something closer to the region of zero.

However, his fans said he was a martyr, and miracle cures were associated with the site of his death, where there soon developed a large pit after people had dug up the earth to take home as souvenirs.

Richard inevitably gets himself killed

On returning home, Richard held a ceremony in Winchester in April 1194, making everyone repeat their homage to him; he then

---

* St. Mary-le-Bow is where the expression 'born within the sound of Bow Bells' comes from, signifying anyone who was a true Londoner rather than a suburbanite who was just pretending. St. Mary-le-Bow is where London's curfew sounded from, calling on everyone to go indoors for the night. And that's why anyone who could hear it was considered a proper Londoner.

† Now in central London and next to Marble Arch Tube station. The last hanging was in 1783, at which point residents in the increasingly swanky part of west London were starting to complain that the gallows with rotting corpses wasn't good for the area's look.

left almost immediately to return to fighting, this time in France, where Philip now had the backing of the Pope. However, the French king ran away, and again four years later had to be rescued from a river as his knights were drowned.

The fun ended for Richard in 1199 when he decided to invade his province of Limousin, in southern France, over a fairly trivial sounding affair: one Achard of Chalus had discovered buried treasure, which apparently included a gold medal showing a Roman emperor and family sitting around a golden table, along with lots of gold coins. Achard refused to let Richard have it, and so the Lionheart besieged the castle, which was defended by only forty men, of whom only two were knights, but who had doggedly refused to surrender.[6]

With characteristic flair and recklessness, King Richard jumped about outside the castle mocking the defenders, until one of them, a teenaged cook, managed to hit him in the shoulder. The wound festered and he died, magnanimous and heroic even in his last breath, asking that his assassin, a poor peasant, be released unharmed (as it was, the orders were ignored and the poor teenager was flayed alive).

Richard, always his mother's favorite, died in her arms—word had been sent after his wound became infected—although according to his supporters the king was still romancing women even on his gangrene-ridden deathbed (which must have been really pleasant for them). He expired after a week of agony, and while his heart was cut out and interred in Normandy, his bowels were buried in Aquitaine as a statement of that country's betrayal of him, as he saw it.

Richard's major legacy is that he took the Norman emblem of two gold lions and added the lion of Aquitaine, using for the first time in 1198 the famous three-lions motif, which has since been associated with cheery and cultured English visitors around Europe since. He also first adopted the phrase *Dieu et mon droit*—'God and my right'—as a battle cry and password, and it was used by later kings to symbolize their (highly dubious) claim to the French throne. Today it is still the motto of the royal family, as well as appearing on the masthead of many institutions such as *The Times* and *Daily Mail*. He's also one of only two English kings to have the honor of being listed as an artist on Spotify, the other being Henry VIII.

During his first trip away, Richard had named Geoffrey's infant son Arthur of Brittany as heir, but forced to choose between the now adolescent nephew and John, the leading figures opted for the latter. Marshal in particular was against Arthur becoming king, stating that he 'has treacherous advisors about him and he is unapproachable and overbearing.' In contrast, the main argument for John was that he was 'a known quantity even if a terrible one.'[7] But as Hubert Walter told Marshal: 'You'll never regret anything in your life so much as you will this.' He wasn't far wrong, and the dispute between Arthur and John would soon be resolved, in a not entirely amicable way.

The Crusades rather fell apart after this. Henry VI of Germany launched a fresh one in 1197 and died almost immediately upon arrival. Then in 1204, the crusaders reached fresh heights of stupidity when on their way to the Holy Land they decided to sack Constantinople, the largest Christian city in the world, after being dragged into one of the Byzantine Empire's vicious power struggles. The Fifth Crusade was even less successful; an attempt to conquer Jerusalem in 1217 led only to the capture of a drinks pot believed to have been used at the wedding of Cana, where Jesus turned water into wine, 'the one and only concrete result of this futile campaign' although crusade leader King Andrew of Hungary, 'who acquired the relic, was as delighted with it as if he had captured Jerusalem itself.'[8] Something like a third of the thirty-two thousand crusaders who traveled east for the adventure died for this great achievement.

The most insane of all was the so-called 'Children's Crusade' of 1212, when thirty-thousand (even the most conservative estimates suggest ten thousand) kids descended on Marseilles in the belief that God would deliver Jerusalem to the Christians 'only if they became children,' taking a Biblical passage way too literally. Most were under twelve, many were begging, and some died on the way; they reached the port city hoping and expecting the sea would divide before them which, alas, it didn't.

Luckily, two merchants turned up, with the entirely trustworthy-sounding names Hugh the Iron and William the Pig, promising to take them to the Middle East, and so the children got onto the ships and they all set sail—and were never heard of again. Years later, however, one or two survivors turned up recounting that they all had all been sold into slavery, and some eighteen of them had ended up being killed in Baghdad for refusing to renounce Christianity. All in all having a crusade comprised entirely of children wasn't the most sensible of ideas.

CHAPTER NINE

Not as Bad as Hitler or Stalin

John has gone down in history as a 'bad king,' but unlike his showy brother, at least he bothered to visit England, he treated the poor no worse than the privileged (equally badly), and as a borderline atheist it is not surprising that he got a bad press from the Church. On the other hand, he did beat his nephew to death in a drunken rage, so nobody's perfect.

Pretty much every notion in history goes through some sort of revisionism, and the more you read into the past the more you realize there are two sides to the story and everything is a blur. Even in John's case there was an attempt to do this in recent years, but it didn't get very far; all the evidence suggests that he was in every way a terrible, terrible man. He was 'clever, insatiably grasping and implacably narcissistic,'[1] according to one modern historian, while Gerald of Wales called John 'a tyrannous whelp' and William of Newburgh said he was 'nature's enemy.' Even one of John's own generals conceded that he was 'a very bad man, cruel and lecherous,' and he was on his payroll.[2] The kindest word comes from twentieth-century historian R. V. Turner, who wrote that 'compared with Hitler and Stalin . . . John seems quite tame'—not exactly a ringing endorsement. Another historian of that period, Osbert Lancaster said of him that 'his sole redeeming feature seems to have been that like so many celebrated criminals, he was invariably kind to his mother.'

Eleanor was forty-five when she brought John into the world, by which time his next youngest sibling was already nine, and while his mother had doted over Richard, she largely ignored John, who seems to be a classic example of the old adage that if you are treated as a child, you behave like one. But Eleanor could hardly be blamed for this, since she had been imprisoned by her husband when John was just six, which probably didn't help his development into a well-rounded human being.

Like his brother, John was a boisterous young boy, and in one charming episode he was having a game of chess, which in those days was played with very heavy pieces (the game had been brought over from the Arab world by the Normans) when he lost his temper and smashed his opponent over the head with the board.[3] This was no different from the behavior of any other members of his family, but John was both violent and a coward.

Already as a youngster he gave the impression of being wrong in the head; in 1185, when John had visited Ireland as its new teenaged despot, he immediately got off to a bad start by making fun of the locals' dress sense and pulling the red beards of Irish kings who came to show him their fealty, a trick that he found immensely amusing; them less so. Having treated the Irish with 'levity and contempt,' he then squandered all his soldiers' pay, much of it on prostitutes and drink during his trip to Waterford, and by the time he was ordered home he'd managed to achieve the impossible by uniting both English soldiers and Irish natives in hating him. John's handling of Ireland was considered so ridiculous that it was reported that Pope Urban III sent the young man a peacock-feathered crown of Ireland to make fun of him.

With his short stature—he was just five feet six inches—and swarthy complexion, he was physically the opposite of his dashing brother.[4] By the time of Magna Carta he had also grown bald and fat, and whatever glamour he possessed in his youth was long gone.

John's career 'was pockmarked by ugly instances of treachery, frivolity and disaster,' and unlike Richard, he was never forgiving or straight in his dealings.[5] His brother had been nicknamed 'Richard yay-or-nay' (i.e., straight answer),[6] but John ignored almost every oath he took, as well as betraying both his father and brother; as soon as he became king he broke alliances with his nephew Otto of Brunswick and the Counts of Flanders and Boulogne. This was a pattern throughout his life, which was partly why Magna Carta had to come about.

He was also cruel and ruthless even compared to his contemporaries, which was a low bar. During John's drunken rages, which were frequent, his face would go dark red and his eyes would blaze and his mouth foam. Most infamous, for some, was his execution of twenty-eight sons of Welsh princes who had rebelled against him, or the way he treated French prisoners of war 'so vilely and in such evil distress that it seemed shameful and ugly to all those who witnessed this cruelty.'[7] John also had the three sons of one baron killed, two of them after being castrated, and on another occasion had a seven-year-old boy hanged.

And he was—at least by modern-day standards—a pedophile.[8]

Still, John was tenderhearted about animals and doted over his pet falcon, Gibbun, who was fed doves, pork, and chicken once a week. So, good in everyone then.

He was also a spendthrift, at a time when most were struggling under huge taxes. John was obsessed with jewels: when he lost a necklace in 1202, a man called Berchal found it and so the king awarded him an annual income of twenty shillings. John even used to publicly wear the coronation regalia of his grandmother Matilda. The king's entourage were so well dressed that even 'his wife's washerwoman wore rabbit fur, paid for from the royal Exchequer,'[9] and he gave generous sick leave to his staff.[10]

To everyone else he was detestable, and during his seventeen-year reign John levied tax after tax to wage war in France, a conflict he lost disastrously. And after his final, humiliating military defeat in 1214, unrest burst into the open and a group of rebel barons defied the king, renouncing homage and fealty. They were led by Robert Fitzwalter, whose daughter the king had supposedly taken some sort of interest in (and not in a good way). What emerged was Magna Carta; a 'failed peace treaty'[11] at the time, but which over the following century would become a firmly established part of English law.

Things start off badly

Within weeks of Richard's death, Arthur's mother, Constance of Brittany, had raised an army with the barons of Anjou and Maine ready to fight. But John got to Rouen first and was therefore made Duke of Normandy and given golden roses as symbol of his power. Along the way, he took a brief detour and sacked the city of Le Mans as punishment for not supporting him. A month later on May 27, he was crowned at Westminster Abbey as King of England. There was a bad omen at John's coronation in Rouen when he dropped the lance that was supposed to represent his office, while his cronies in the congregation sniggered. Also, his wife was not invited, which was not a good sign.

In order to secure the throne, John made what was regarded as a shameful peace treaty in May 1200, paying homage to Philip. The idea of homage was a formality, and the kings of France never asked the Angevins for any actual money in the past, as their supposed underlings were in reality as powerful as them. But at Le Goulet, John had agreed to pay tribute, a bad deal that earned him the nickname 'Softsword.' As part of the peace, John gave southern Normandy to the King of France in the hope he would leave him alone.[12] The deal also stated that Philip's son Louis was to marry one of John's nieces in Spain, and so Eleanor of Aquitaine, now in her midseventies, set off across France to collect the girl, passing snow drifts in the Pyrenees during a thousand-mile trip.[13]

But John was soon in conflict with the French. The king had grown bored with his wife, Isabel of Gloucester, who was too closely related to him for marriage, and although Henry II had just ignored this problem, now that he had become king John decided he wanted another wife. In fact, poor Isabel was so obscure and ignored that Roger of Howden, the main court chronicler at the time, couldn't even get her name right and kept on referring to her as Hawise, while others called her Joan or Eleanor.[14]

John chose Isabella of Angoulême, who apart from being a child and already engaged, was a perfect choice. The marriage between Isabella and Hugh 'le Brun' of Lusignan, Lord of La Marche, was supposed to bring peace to two warring provinces in western France, but not everyone was pleased by the prospect; once united, these two lands could present a threat to John's empire, placed right in the middle of his French territory, so he wasn't entirely thinking with his crotch when he spoiled their marriage. What exactly happened is unclear as testimony is colored by the fact that everyone hated John. According to one story, John first saw his second wife as she was being led to the church by her father—and, as overlord, stopped it and married her himself, which must have really spoiled the wedding; this sounds slightly like implausible propaganda.

But what was true and shocking, or at least noteworthy, was her youth, because of which Hugh de Lusignan had postponed the wedding. Isabella was very young, perhaps only twelve but maybe even younger (her parents were first recorded as married in 1191 and her first child did not arrive until 1207), while John was in his thirties. However, the Benedictine monk Matthew Paris didn't think her entirely blameless, stating that 'she should have been named Jezebel rather than Isabel' because she had enticed the monarch, which to modern ears doesn't present Matthew in an entirely sympathetic light.

Some people were rather upset about all this; John had agreed to marry a Portuguese princess so they weren't too happy about him characteristically going back on his word. In fact, John had sent envoys off to arrange the marriage in Portugal only for his representatives to return home to find he had married someone else.

Although some historians say the marriage was rather a good move politically, and reasonable, it's agreed that not compensating the Lusignans was outrageous. Instead, when there was discontent in Poitou over this rather inconsiderate behavior, John ordered his officials to harry the Lusignans and 'do them all the harm they could' (as a general rule of thumb when picturing events just imagine John as Alan Rickman playing the Sheriff of Nottingham in *Robin Hood: Prince of Thieves*).

As for his first wife, she had brought most of south Wales as a dowry, which John simply kept.

The Lusignans appealed to King Philip, who was overlord to John as well as Hugh. In terms of sexual morality, the French king was at the other end of the spectrum to his Angevin rival, and was certainly not impressed by John's behavior. In 1193, as part of his ill-conceived Viking revival invasion, Philip had married a Danish princess called Ingeberg who was said to be as beautiful as Helen of Troy, but after one night together he decided he wanted to divorce her. Why, we'll never know. The Pope denied his request, but the king still refused to have marital relations with her—for the next sixteen years. Only when Philip needed the pontiff's support for an invasion of England did he agree to do the deed; the royal bedding led to joyous national celebration and street parties. Ingeberg must have felt just *brilliant* about all this.

Philip now chose to punish John, who promised to attend a hearing on April 28, 1202, and to hand over two castles as security; obviously he had no intention of doing either. In the meantime, John seized the lands of leading lords in Poitou, charged them with treason, and then suggested it should be resolved with trial by battle, with him using professional champions (he was obviously not going to fight himself); they refused and looked to the king of France for help.

When John failed to appear at the hearing, Philip declared him a 'contumacious vassal' who had forfeited Aquitaine, Poitou, and Anjou. Philip also knighted Arthur, who in July 1202 did homage to him for Henry II's lands. Now French soldiers invaded Normandy, while Lusignan and the other Poitevin barons were joined by Prince Arthur who now—bizarrely—besieged his own grandmother Eleanor at Mirebeau Castle, outside Poitiers.

John turned up and took the rebels captive, and although Arthur initially escaped, one of John's loyal sidekicks, William des Roches, eventually caught him. The outspoken adolescent, who by all accounts sounded as awful as the rest of the family, demanded he be made King of England although by now he was hardly in a position to ask for much.

When he came to the throne, John had sworn to agree that he, his lieutenant William des Roches, and Arthur 'would all be good friends,' all of this 'firmly promised . . . in good faith.' However, although the victory at Mirebeau had been the work of des Roches, John soon alienated him and—'puffed up with pride which daily grew and that so blurred his vision that he could not see reason'—behaved in a way that 'he lost the affection of the barons of the land.'[15] Worst of all was John's appalling treatment of the prisoners there who were kept in chains at the prisons, which led des Roches to abandon John and join Philip that year.

John then invited his nephew around for talks in his castle; things obviously got out of hand and Arthur's body was seen floating in the Seine a couple of days later. He might have jumped out of a tower, or John may have crushed Arthur's head with a stone after flying off the handle when the young lad had denounced his 'usurpation.' Either way, it wasn't a good week for him. There were also rumors in England that Arthur had been blinded and castrated, or at least John had ordered the mutilation, which had been disobeyed, or that his underlings had carried out a cold-blooded execution; English opinion was horrified by John's treatment of a relation who was barely an adult.

John was now ordered by Philip to come to Paris to explain Arthur's disappearance. He refused. King John then managed to lose the whole of Normandy in spectacular fashion, running away after Philip had taken his major fortress, whereas his brother would have dug in and produced something suitably spectacular, perhaps while sticking his hand down a lion's throat. In March 1204, after months of siege during which John refused to lift a finger, Richard's great Norman castle of Chateau Gaillard fell to the French, after being bravely defended by Roger de Lacy. The invaders had taken it after sneaking in through the latrines, so we must hope they were well rewarded, although Philip once said of his own men invading Normandy that they were like 'toilet rags' to be 'used and disposed of down the latrine when one had had one's use of them.'[16] At the time, John was far away, busy 'giving orders for his horses and hounds and falcons to be dispatched to Normandy in preparation for his coming' so that he could hunt when he finally bothered to arrive.[17]

John had an army as large as his rival's, but he still miraculously lost. One reason was that since he basically had no money left and didn't want to pay them, John had allowed his Angevin mercenaries to treat Normandy like conquered territory and plunder it at will, breaking all the rules of feudalism, not to mention basic common sense. Not surprisingly, the Normans weren't desperately keen to fight for him, and when in August 1204 he lost Normandy altogether the French soldiers were welcomed. 'King John lost the love of his people here in Normandy,' wrote a contemporary, 'because that wolf Lupescar [the most hated of the mercenary captains] treated them as though he were in enemy territory.'

To make matters worse at home, many of his French henchmen came over to England with him, and he rewarded them with great jobs. Some of them were basically murderers (one, Peter de Maulay, had supposedly killed Arthur) but were given estates in the kingdom. De Maulay got a castle in Dorset and a marriage that brought him the whole of Doncaster. This was one more source of resentment, and would become one of the issues at stake in Magna Carta, with five of the clauses dealing with these 'alien knights.'

The capture of Normandy, which increased the French crown's income by 70 percent,[18] would help make France the supreme European power for hundreds of years.* After Philip's victory, only Gascony—the southern portion of Aquitaine—was left of the Crown's French possessions, and English-born Norman barons now had a dilemma: were they English or French? Philip was first to issue an order confiscating the lands of Normans who stayed in England and John followed soon after. Although many aristocrats lost possessions, it was much worse for their tenants who faced the uncertainty of a new lord who may well have been hostile to their old one, and to them.

Most Anglo-Norman aristocrats grew up in England and were cared for by English nannies and servants, and by the third generation most were marrying English or part-English girls. The barons may have spoken French for official business, but many now conversed in English at home, and all were fluent by the 1170s. Meanwhile, their version of French had become detached from that which was spoken in Paris and had become a subject of mockery. English people were already back then known for speaking French badly, even when French was for many of them their first language; 'Marlborough French' was, according to Walter Map, so called because in that town 'there is a spring of which they say that whoever tastes it speaks bad French.'

---

*   This supremacy lasted up until the eighteenth century when a British officer by the name of George Washington started a war in 1756, the year 1759 being seen as the start of the British era.

Had it not been for John's disastrous rule, then England might have stayed attached to a continental, French-speaking empire. And without a large empire, John was now forced to spend all his time in England micromanaging things; as Abbot Ralph of the Cistercian House of Coggeshall in Essex was to note, 'this king governed indefatigably.' In fact, by most accounts he was an effective administrator, if one could overlook the torture, murder, and rape.

John also fell out with Marshal, who alone refused to give up his land in Normandy and did homage to the French king for it. John was obviously angry about this, but Marshal was the only person who could get away with it. Afterwards, they were on bad terms, and later John had his fifteen-year-old son William taken into his care, basically as a hostage.

In 1205, John threatened the French king that he was going to invade with an 'unbelievably large' force, and so he raised an invasion force at Portsmouth on the south coast, but it ended up a comical disaster. Having arranged a huge fleet, John confronted Marshal for having sworn homage to Philip. Marshal offered to do trial by combat with anyone who would call him a traitor in front of all the assembled 'barons and bachelors,' but there was an awkward silence as no one would challenge him to a fight.

Then the fleet mutinied and refused to join John on an invasion of France, and so in a huff he sailed around the Isle of Wight until he calmed down, leaving everyone to think he had left for a suicide mission in France.

Drink!

John was a very bad man, but one of the upsides of his paranoia was that the atmosphere of suspicion it created led to a huge increase in the number of legal documents. One mysterious record of the time shows a pipe roll from 1210 concerning a baron, that: 'Robert de Vaux owes five of the best horses so that the King should shut his mouth about the wife of Henry Pinel.' Charming man, the king. Another states that the 'wife of Hugh de Neville offers the king 200 chickens so that she may lie one night with her husband.' It either suggested that the king's duties were taking Hugh away from his wife or that the king was forcing himself on her. Or that she was his mistress and this was a joke at Hugh's expense.

Hugh de Neville had been one of Richard's comrades in Palestine and had grown friendly with John, becoming a gambling and drinking pal. John eventually placed his wife at the de Neville's home, Marlborough Castle, even though his first wife happened to also be living there. It must have been fantastically awkward. John spent a week at Marlborough for Christmas 1204, during which two tuns of wine—1,900 liters—were consumed.

John surrounded himself with cronies in his mold, men who were as financially ravenous as him, and de Neville fitted the bill; as chief forester, he was in charge of one-third of all land in the realm, and would force prisoners to sign and seal documents agreeing to awful punishments if they disobeyed him. Likewise, his royal chancellor, former Bishop of Durham Richard Marsh, who like John was drunk most of the time, would force monasteries to issue blank charters, sealed already so that the king could make any demand he wished to, the medieval equivalent of a blank check.

John's reputation for cruelty and sexual wrongdoing is well established, including his habit of forcing himself on the wives and daughters of noblemen. The most serious accusation involved the wife of Eustace de Vesci, serious because de Vesci was the most powerful baron in the far north of England, and would become John's nemesis. The son of a Norman landholder, husband of the King of Scotland's bastard daughter, and Richard's old companion in war, de Vesci accused John of raping his wife, and when John came to visit his home the story goes that a prostitute was put in his spouse's bed just in case John came in at night—which he did.

Despite this, John could also be quite jealous. The chief guardian of the queen was a man called 'Terry the German,' who sounds like some ludicrous East End villain from a British gangster film. In 1207, the king wrote to Terry from France, stating: 'Know that we are well and unharmed, and . . . we shall shortly be coming to your parts, and we shall be thinking of you like a hawk. And although we may have been absent for ten years, when we come to you it shall seem to us as if we had been away no more than three days. Take care of the thing entrusted to you, letting us know frequently how it fares.' The 'thing' or 'it' was John's wife, and the letter was probably an unsubtle warning to anyone thinking of getting too close to the queen that something unspeakably bad would happen to them as a result. John had half a dozen or so illegitimate children by various mistresses, but this wasn't especially scandalous by the standards of the age, and was positively restrained compared to his father. Terry the German was later in November 1214 ordered to take Isabella to Gloucester and 'keep her there in the chamber in which our daughter Joan was born.'

Still, despite all these faults, John had a great sense of humor. In 1212, the king made his courtiers sign a document stating that should one Peter de Maulay cause the king offense, the Earl of Cornwall's son would be whipped and the Earl of Salisbury's hawks would all be confiscated. This was considered very funny by the king, and was typical of his dry wit.

However, John's temper was notorious, and could inflame in seconds and disappear just as quickly. Richard of Devizes described his mood as 'wrath cut furrows across his forehead; his burning eyes shot sparks; rage darkened the ruddy color of his face.' Closely related to his cruelty and violence was John's massive drinking problem. As a basic rule, everyone in medieval Europe was drunk most of the time, with the typical English peasant consuming on average eight pints of beer per day.[19] There was often no clean water to drink in cities, and it was not until the seventeenth century that coffee and tea brought alternatives to slowly getting off one's face all day long. Besides which, few people had jobs that required intellect and sobriety and life was pretty awful when sober.

Beer at the time would have been absolutely disgusting, close to the texture of porridge as it wasn't until the fourteenth century that hops were introduced from the Low Countries, after which the drink would have first resembled what we now think of as beer. Not even the most daring hipster has ever tried to recreate thirteenth-century ale as a statement of irony or quirkiness. Without hops, the beer also went-production off very quickly, and so large-scale brewing was not possible, most of it being done in houses; it didn't matter as people drank it very quickly just to blot out life.

Wine, meanwhile, which was transported in 252-gallon wooden casks at the time, mostly came from southwest France, with English wine-production disappearing due to climate change, but even the stuff consumed by the royal family was grim. Peter of Blois wrote of the wine at Henry's II court that it 'turned sour and moldy, thick, greasy, stale, flat and smacking of pitch.' He said: 'I have sometimes seen great lords served with wine so muddy that a man must need [to] close his eyes and clench his teeth, wry-mouthed and shuddering, and filtering the stuff rather than drinking it.'[20]

Not that most English people cared about the quality. As early as the eighth century, St. Boniface had mentioned the national problem with drink, including among clergy, calling it 'a vice peculiar to the heathens [Vikings] and to our race, and that neither Franks, Gauls, Lombards, Romans nor Greeks indulge in.' Few things change. Richard FitzNigel, Bishop of Ely and head of the treasury at the time of Henry II, said the English were 'natural drunks,' and court rolls from the period are full of tragicomic misadventures involving ale, illiterate peasants, and agricultural instruments. Twelfth-century writer William of Malmesbury said of the English that 'Drinking in parties was an universal practice, in which occupation they passed entire nights as well as days.'

Jacques de Vitry, a theologian and cardinal who lived in Paris at the end of the twelfth century, described 'the distinctive characteristics of each nation: the French were proud and womanish; the Germans furious and obscene; the Lombards greedy, malicious, and cowardly; and the English were drunkards and had tails.'* The Franciscan Salimbene noticed that it was the Englishman's habit always to drain off a beaker of wine, saying 'he bi a vu' (I drink to you), implying that his friend must drink as much as he, and he 'taketh it exceedingly ill if any do otherwise than he himself hath taught in word and shown by example.'[21]

In this period, England went through one of its periodic booze epidemics, so that 'the whole land was filled with drink and drinkers.' By the end of the century, 354 drinking establishments were in London, and everyone drank heavily, although they did so among their own class—the wealthy drank in inns, the middle ranks in taverns, while at the bottom of the social ladder there were the alehouses, where violence was almost guaranteed.

At 'church ales' money was raised for the upkeep of the parish by hosting marathon boozing sessions in which parishioners were encouraged to drink as much as possible. These events could go on for three days, and after a certain time bachelors who were still able to stand were allowed to drink for free. Weddings were also extremely drunken, so much so that in 1223 Richard Poore, Bishop of Salisbury, was forced to make a proclamation that marriages must be sober, and 'celebrated reverently and with honor, not with laughter

---

* The idea that Englishmen had tails was apparently quite common on the continent and supposedly went back to St. Augustine who arrived in 597 to convert the pagan Anglo-Saxons. He found they fastened cows' tails to the back of their clothes because they thought it looked good. And so as punishment for this vanity, they and their descendents were doomed to always have tails. That's why I'm writing this on a special chair.

or sport or at public potations or feasts.' Not that churchmen were much better, especially as they did much of the brewing. Cistercian monks at Fountains Abbey in Yorkshire produced 1,100 gallons (five thousand liters) of ale every week, both for consumption and sale, and fitting in with medieval stereotypes some clerics were inebriated quite often. A chronicle composed at Ely cathedral recalls a priest so drunk he could barely walk, but who after trying to perform Mass vomited and defecated in front of the congregation.

The worst drink-related incident occurred in 1212 when London Bridge burned down after a 'Scot-ale,' with up to three thousand charred or drowned bodies turning up on the banks of the river the following morning. Scot-ales were bring-your-own-bottle events where 'the highest credit was accorded to him who made the most of his fellows drunk and himself emptied the largest tankards.'[22] Inevitably, this combination or rancid alcohol and ill-judged horseplay often ended badly.

Leading the way in this national drinking marathon was King John, who even by the standards of the time was pretty exceptional all the same, keeping an estimated 180,000 gallons of wine at his disposal, which some might say was a slight hint of alcoholism. John's butler was personally responsible for ensuring a tun (240 gallons) or two of wine was waiting for him at his next stop, wherever he was.

CHAPTER TEN

John vs. God

As the youngest son, John, may originally have been destined for the Church, and had his elder brothers not gotten themselves killed, he might have stayed there, although it cannot be said he would have been a very conscientious cleric. At the age of one, he was sent to an abbey to live with monks but was eventually found to be woefully unsuited to the life of prayer and reflection. However, he did retain a love of books throughout his life; and indeed, in 1203 when he should have been worrying about Normandy falling to the French, he had his library sent across to him so he could spend some time reading.

John might not have even believed in God, and certainly treated oaths in a way that suggests not. He apparently did not take Holy Communion after childhood, nor did he receive it at his coronation, which was considered shocking for the time. He openly ate meat on Fridays and hunted on feast days, blatantly breaking religious rules. Like his father, he found attending church unbelievably boring and he didn't even pretend to make an effort. On one Easter Mass, when the very holy St. Hugh of Lincoln was giving the homily, John sent the bishop three notes telling him to hurry so he could go to lunch. During services he was forced to attend, he'd take out a gold coin at collection time, ostentatiously play with it, then put it back in his purse.* In another example of his not-very-great respect for religion, when his half brother Archbishop Geoffrey of York visited in 1207 to appeal against a heavy tax, the cleric threw himself at John's feet. John then threw himself at Geoffrey's feet in return and cried 'Look, Lord Archbishop, I'm doing just what you did!' Then he laughed his head off.

The only cleric he had any respect for, indeed the only person who seemed to bring out any humanity in the man, was the saintly Hugh of Lincoln,† who the king admired so much he sat by him on his deathbed and helped carry his coffin; John founded Beaulieu Abbey in the New Forest in his honor—but that was something of a blip. And while John might have been an nonbeliever, he wasn't entirely rational, and wore a jewel around his neck that he was convinced would bring him victory in France, which it didn't.

Having made enemies everywhere, the king now fell out with the Church over the choice of Archbishop of Canterbury. In 1205, Archbishop Hubert Walter passed away following a fever caused by an infected carbuncle (people died of the strangest things back then). John is supposed to have cried in delight 'By God's feet! Now for the first time I am king and lord of England.'[1]

He wanted his crony John de Gray to be given the post, but Pope Innocent III insisted on Stephen Langton, who turned out to be a formidable and influential figure in the Magna Carta story, and an unsung hero of English liberty; he was, however, blatantly unsuited to the job, his main claim being that he was the Pope's former tutor. To intellectual circles Langton was a great choice, being a figure of theological distinction; John, however, did not move in intellectual circles. On top of this, Langton had taught at Paris for

---

*   Fans of British comedy will of course recognize this behavior from Edmund Blackadder.

†   He is literally a saint, and is one of the few genuinely sympathetic figures of the period, saving the Jews of Lincoln from a massacre.

twenty years and John had become extremely hostile to anything French. He refused the nomination.

Despite the king's insistence, the Pope appointed Langton anyway, and so John declared that anyone who recognized the appointment was a public enemy.

In June 1207, after the Pope had consecrated Langton, the king responded by sending notorious mercenary crossbowmen to Christ Church, Canterbury, to intimidate the monks; as a result most fled abroad.[2]

The papacy, in response, issued an interdict, under which all Church services in the country were suspended; church bells were not rung, and Christian marriages could not be properly made. For John, not an especially pious man, this was about as much of a punishment as a parent threatening to stop taking their child to church.

And for the king, it also had the added bonus that he could collect the revenue from all the churches, a huge amount of money. Then John confiscated all clerical assets on the grounds that they weren't doing their jobs, and imprisoned the priests' mistresses and demanded cash for their return; obviously, as he well knew, the clergy didn't want to make a big fuss about this and most simply paid up. For the common people, although baptisms and last rites were still performed, Mass had to be practiced outside, as priests wouldn't cross the picket line. As a result of the interdict, people were buried in ditches and church piss-ups had to be done in the porch rather than inside the building. Marriages continued, sometimes at church doors, but there were no wedding Masses. Still, though the king wasn't popular, there was not a single protest about Mass not being said during the interdict, which suggests that most people weren't that bothered about it either; they probably regarded it as a chance to get another hour's drinking in. In fact, there was such enthusiastic support for John's anti-clerical policy that he had to issue 'instructions that anyone who did or spoke evil against the religious or secular clergy was to be hanged to the nearest oak tree.'[3] On the other hand, one story recounts how John met by the road some officers who took away a man who had murdered a priest, at which point the king ordered him to be freed because 'he has killed one of my enemies.'[4]

There's some anecdotal evidence that many people didn't seem to have been that serious about religion at the time; one preacher, Alexander Ashby, complained that at the solemn moment of the Mass when 'the priest prayed silently before consecrating the Eucharist, a hubbub of gossip and joking commonly broke out among the congregation.'

The interdict had one long-lasting effect, however. England's first university, Oxford, had originated around 1100, growing out of two monastic settlements at nearby Woodstock. But in 1209, fighting broke out between locals and students after one of the latter was accused of murdering a local woman. The townies couldn't find him so the mayor put three fellow students in jail and 'after a few days . . . these clerks were led out from the city and hanged'—lynched effectively. As a result, many scholars left the city, but because of the interdict many of the clerics who ran the university had already fled Oxford and, with the atmosphere decidedly hostile, they decided not to bother returning and instead relocated to a small town to the east in the middle of a bog—called Cambridge.[5]

Such students vs. locals conflict was common in the Middle Ages, and by today's standards absurdly violent, brawls often ending in multiple fatalities. Overall, more than two hundred incidents of murder and serious violence occurred at Oxford university between 1209 and 1399.[6] A few years after the 1209 incident, there was trouble when the mayor of Oxford ordered all 'Lewd Women then in Gaol' to be expelled from town. It was all, apparently, the fault of 'French students whose infamous Lust had engag'd them in their Quarrels, and by haunting Stewes and Brothels, had contracted the foul Diseases.' This led the Pope's representative in England to visit the town and 'hither to reform the Corruptions of the Place.' The students went to see the legate to complain but were rudely told to go away by the porter 'in his loud Italian voice,' which seemed to annoy them further, so they forced their way in. A fight broke out and a cook who had thrown boiling water over one of the students was killed.

There was also frequent mob violence among students, including one incident of fighting between 'Northern English and the Welsh' on the one hand, and the 'Southern English,' each side flying banners, in which 'divers on both sides [were] slain and pitifully wounded.' Then in 1298 on the feast of St. Mathias (February 24), a fight occurred after the city bailiff was attacked by some students and it escalated so that on the following day students 'took all the lay-folk they could find, beat them and wickedly trampled on them,' killing one and wounding many by a church altar.

The most notorious was the St. Scholastica Day riot of 1355, in which a dispute between two students and an innkeeper led to forty-eight hours of disorder and the deaths of thirty locals and sixty-three scholars. This had started after some students had thrown their drink at an innkeeper's face; apparently they had been served 'indifferent wine' at the Swyndlestock Tavern after which the vintner gave them 'stubborn and saucy language.' Then the town folk attacked the students, 'some with bows and arrows, others with divers weapons,' and fighting broke out again the following morning. The entire faculty fled after 'some innocent wretches' were killed and 'scornfully cast into the house of easement'—the toilet—a deed done by 'diabolical imps.' Those who were injured limped away 'carrying their entrails in their hands in a most lamentable manner.'*

---

* The last big Oxford university fight was in 1389 between English and Welsh scholars, the former shouting 'War, war, sle, sle, sle, the Welsh doggys and her whelps and ho so looketh out of his howese, he shall in good sorte be dead.' Cambridge also had numerous brawls, including major incidents in 1261, 1381, and 1417, when the scholars 'armed in a warlike manner, caused great terror to the mayor, by laying in wait to kill him and his officers.'

Not that medieval Oxford was just about fighting; they also did some learning there. The most important of the thirteenth-century scholars was the Somerset-born Roger Bacon, who had studied at Paris before coming to Oxford in 1250. He is sometimes credited with being the first European to advocate the modern scientific method, brought from ancient Greece via the Arab world, although inevitably he ended up getting in trouble with the Church and spent much of his later years under a sort of house arrest.*

John also annoyed the Church by giving his support to the Cathars, the heretics of southern France who had developed an extremely austere religion that was anti-meat, anti-sex, and basically anti-everything fun, and who were mercilessly punished in the Albigensian crusade.† It was rumored that opponents of the monarch wanted to replace King John with the crusade's leader, the fanatical Catholic maniac Simon de Montfort; nothing came of it, but his son would play a big part in English history. Such was John's lack of belief that there was even an improbable story that he had sent secret messages 'to the emir of Morocco to tell him that he would

---

* Most curiously, Bacon predicted in 1250 that one day 'by the figurations of art there be made instruments of navigation without men to row them, as great ships to brooke the sea, only with one man to steer them, and they shall sail far more swiftly than if they were full of men; also chariots that shall move with unspeakable force without any living creature to stir them. Likewise an instrument may be made to fly withall if one sits in the midst of the instrument, and do turn an engine, by which the wings, being artificially composed, may beat the air after the manner of a flying bird.'

† The crusade was most famous for the response the leader gave when told lots of people they were massacring at Beziers would be Catholic rather than heretical Cathars: 'Kill Them All, God will know his own.' Between 7-15,000 civilians were killed in the massacre which, in fairness, was not the Church's greatest moment.

voluntarily give up himself and his kingdom and also abandon the Christian faith' in return for an alliance. This is unlikely in the extreme, and anyway, if John was interested in converting to Islam, he certainly hadn't read the part about abstaining from alcohol.

John promised, in 1208, that if any clerics arrived from Rome, even the Pope, he would send them back with their noses slit and eyes gouged out.[7] Meanwhile, the king's profits from the interdict of £100,000 were spent on things such as new costumes for the king's pet lion and its keeper 'and two thousand crossbow bolts and military uniforms.'[8] The Pope did not approve, and now excommunicated John, which bothered him not in the slightest: 'He neither feared God nor regarded man; it was as if he alone were mighty upon the earth,' a monk in Canterbury lamented. Again in 1211, John said he'd hang Langton if he returned to England. One priest, Geoffrey of Norwich, read a letter from the Pope stating that a clergyman did not owe loyalty to anyone who had been excommunicated, so John had him wrapped in lead, killing him.[9]

However, the excommunication led to increasing paranoia, and on March 17, 1208, there was a muster of the fleet at London. The king ordered that all English seamen abroad should come home 'with the threat of dire consequences if they refused his summons.'[10] The following week, he ordered that all foreign ships be seized except those from Denmark and Norway, the only countries he thought weren't against him. He also ordered that all leading barons hand over family members as hostages.

Among the most unpopular things John did was to keep his barons in permanent debt to him, mostly through arbitrary taxes and payments he seemed to make up on the spot. What made him especially unpopular was the issue of inheritance, and the 'relief' that had to be handed over, which violated Henry I's promise of a reasonable tax. John would suddenly announce that a baron had to pay off all his debts, leaving him effectively bankrupt overnight; if they refused, he would take a family member. In perhaps the most

notorious incident, John turned against the baron William de Briouze, paranoid about his loyalty and demanding £3,500 from him
as immediate payment.

De Briouze was one of the most prominent of the marcher lords,
the semi-independent Norman aristocrats who controlled the border ('march') with Wales. William owned vast amounts of land in
Normandy, Wales, England, and Ireland, while his wife, 'Matilda of
Hay' as John called her, was an even more impressive figure, virtually ruling the border region single-handedly from her castle, and at
one point fighting off a Welsh invasion; she owned twelve thousand
cows, and boasted she could feed an army with them.*

William de Briouze had been a loyal follower of John, and was
involved in capturing Arthur, but he had also refused or delayed
paying money he owed the king and may even have used violence
against royal officials who demanded it. However, the amount John
asked for was vast and unaffordable. And when John's men came
to their castle demanding a hostage, Mrs. de Briouze made a terrible mistake. 'With the sauciness of a woman,' says the chronicler
Roger Wendover, she refused to hand over a child, saying, 'I will not
deliver up my sons to your lord, King John, for he basely murdered
his nephew, Arthur.' As a general piece of advice to medieval wives:
if your husband's boss has murdered his nephew in a drunken rage,
best not to bring it up in an argument.

The de Briouzes all fled to Ireland, and in pursuit John launched
an armada of seven hundred ships from west Wales, with eight hundred
knights ready to be transported across the Irish Sea for his vindictive
campaign. Meanwhile, the de Briouze family lands in Wales and
were harried by John's sheriff of Gloucester.[11] After John's forces had
besieged a castle they were staying in, Matilda and her son William

---

* Matilda is perhaps most famous in the public mind as the subject of
  the bestselling romance novel *Lady of Hay*, in which she is reincarnated
  in the twentieth century and works in publishing.

fled to Scotland where they were captured by a local warlord, Duncan of Carrick, who was distantly related to John through his great-grandfather Henry I. The king had Matilda and her eldest son William locked up and left to die in Corfe Castle, Dorset, and in an especially gruesome twist their bodies were found together, with bite marks on the son's cheeks where his starving, crazed mother had tried to eat him. The elder William fled to France where he died not longer after.

Things like that tended to tarnish John's reputation, and he issued an unusual sort of press release 'so that there should be an authoritative statement of the truth.' It wasn't so much an apology or explanation as a warning 'to demonstrate the utter ruin awaiting those who cross the king.'[12]

Over this William Marshal, who had links with de Briouze, further fell out with the king, who took him for a traitor and so held his son hostage and confiscated his castles. However, that year the king's representative in Ireland, Meiler FitzHenry, of 'dark complexion, with black eyes and a stern, piercing look,' whose father was also one of Henry I's bastards, attacked Marshal's lands while he was in England, and John told Marshal about the news 'with a laugh,' clearly being behind it. There followed a mini-war between Meiler and Marshal's people, with twenty people killed at the settlement of New Ross, but eventually the heroic former tournament champion won. The King was 'not amused at all,' but Marshal remained in Ireland, keeping his head down.

In 1209, John became so paranoid that he decided to make everyone come to Marlborough castle to swear allegiance to him. Gervase of Canterbury wrote of the event in September: 'All the men in England, rich and poor and middling, aged fifteen and upwards, came together at Marlborough on the king's orders, and there they swore fealty, both to the king and to his son, Henry,' who was now two years old. At the end of the ceremony, John gave a kiss of peace to the Crown, which according to one historian was 'one of the earliest air kisses to be recorded in English history.'[13]

Now tax went up by 300 percent, a policy that unsurprisingly wasn't very popular; John also went to Oxford to meet barons and demanded 'scuttage,' or 'shield tax,' the payment of money by barons as a substitute for doing military service in defense of Normandy. Yet many Anglo-Norman aristocrats no longer had lands across the Channel, and saw little reason why they should bother helping.

No means of raising revenue were left untapped; King John even sold immunity from lawsuits at the shire courts, demanded scuttage for nonexistent battles, and added 'gracious aids' (i.e., taxes) on personal goods.

In 1210, John announced a fine of £44,000 from the country's small Jewish community, and also took to torturing Jews to raise money, taking a tooth a day out of one Bristol resident until he handed over a vast fortune of £6,666—the poor man gave up after the seventh. The century saw increased persecution of England's Jewish population, which had always relied on the protection of the monarch against the Christian majority, who were often heavily indebted to Jewish moneylenders. Popular hysteria was partly fueled by the growth of a genre of conspiracy theory in which Jews ritually murdered Christian children. The rumors were started by cretinous peasants in 1144 with a story that a boy called William, had been abducted and killed, although it later transpired he didn't exist. After William, various other similarly nonexistent boys went missing, and the position of the Church also hardened. From 1218, all Jews had to wear a badge, and four years later Jews were banned from employing Christian women or building any new synagogues. In 1244, Jewish books were burned and the Dominican order took to actively persecuting Jews, who were also expelled from different towns after popular petitions.

To be fair to John, he was not a religious bigot, and had no interest in persecuting heretics—he only did it out of sheer greed and a more general lack of humanity. In fact, he also persecuted Christian clergy from 1210 demanding the Cistercians hand over a load of cash, because they were known to be rich. Some houses, such as Meaux Abbey in Yorkshire and Waverley Abbey in Surrey, had to close because of the fines John imposed. In Norfolk, Jews and Cistercians were seen going together door-to-door begging for food.

The dispute with the Church was only resolved when the King of France threatened to invade, with the Pope's support. John was now in a terrible pickle, but Marshal rescued him by getting twenty-seven Irish barons to swear an oath of loyalty saying that they were 'prepared to live or die with the king and that till the last they would faithfully and inseparably adhere to him.' Marshal was recalled to England, and suggested making peace with the Pope. He was cynical about the Vatican, and his *History* was scathing about the corruption there, saying that envoys to Rome only had to come with the relics of St. Gold and St. Silver, those 'worthy martyrs in the eyes of Rome.' Peter of Capua, the papal legate, was, in Marshal's view, 'incredibly adept in the arts of trickery and subterfuge' with a face 'more yellow than a kite's claw.'

John used the money he had amassed to start wars with the Welsh, Irish, and Scots, invading each country between 1209 and 1210. In August 1209, he had marched to Scotland with thirteen thousand Welsh foot soldiers, fifteen hundred English knights, and seven thousand crossbowmen and Brabantine mercenaries from the Low Countries, who were notorious for their cruelty. Scotland's feeble, elderly King William agreed to pay 15,000 marks 'for having the king's goodwill' and gave his two daughters over to John as hostages, as well as his fourteen-year-old son Alexander, who John could marry to whomever he wanted as long as it wasn't to someone of lowly status.

He also turned against Llywelyn the Great of Wales, despite his being married to John's illegitimate daughter, Joan (not to be confused with his other daughter, Joan), because of his alliance with de Briouze. In July 1210, John invaded the country and the bishop of Bangor refused to meet him because he was excommunicated, so John burned the city down and had the churchman seized in his cathedral. In a rather unmanly way, Llywelyn sent his wife to sue for peace, as he was 'unable to bear the king's cruelty.' The Welsh leader had to pay a huge price for defeat, with everything east of the Conwy surrendered to England 'forever.' A single line from the annals of Margam Abbey in Wales describes what happened to those Welshman in John's hands: 'Twenty-two of the noblest and strongest in arms were starved to death in Corfe Castle, so that not one of them escaped.'

John was pretty good at fighting battles against weak Celtic mountain warlords, but when faced with anything harder he caved in, and this is what soon happened.

CHAPTER ELEVEN

The Northerners

John was a monster, and possibly unhinged. However, in medieval times people would generally go along with the king, however mad or rapacious he was, as long as he kept winning battles, and unfortunately John wasn't very good at this.

By the summer of 1212, such was his unpopularity that the king had to hurry back from Wales to deal with rumors of a plot of his death. In his paranoia, he summoned six knights from every county to attend Court, ironically a procedure that would become one of the barons' demands in the following decades and eventually form the basis of the House of Commons. The king concluded that Eustace de Vesci and Robert Fitzwalter—a major landowner in Essex—were planning to murder him; it had been rumored that the king wished to seduce Fitzwalter's daughter and this may have been a motive. Whether they were planning his death or not, he now made them his enemies, and the men fled to France and Scotland respectively. Fitzwalter and John had another old score to settle; Fitzwalter's son-in-law Geoffrey de Mandeville had killed a servant of William Brewer, one of John's officials, in a brawl over lodgings while they were in the king's entourage. When John proposed hanging him (quite reasonably, really), Fitzwalter threatened to raise an army of two thousand knights to defy the monarch.

The king became increasingly deranged, developing a life-style that would have been familiar to Stalin or Saddam Hussein. He refused to sleep outside of a royal castle, although as he had acquired some fifty of them, this made his paranoia easier. He never spent more than three days in the same building, terrified that his barons might betray him, which to be fair they probably would, but he still put enormous sums into having these residences maintained. Although the king was a late riser, sleeping until almost midday, he'd arrange for his baggage train—loaded with gallons of wine—to go on before first light.

Because of his paranoia, and the fact that he had so many people locked up in various dungeons, John developed a complex code to be used when he wished orders to be carried out. In fact, it was so complex he sometimes forgot the right passwords himself. (A dilemma many in the twenty-first century would sympathize with.)

That year, while on tour in the north, John was told that a hermit called Peter of Wakefield, 'a fanatical rustic who lived on bread and water,' prophesized that he would not make his fourteenth anniversary in charge, and so John had him arrested, along with his son.[1]

In the summer in Cornwall, two of the king's underlings, Alan de Dunstanville and Henry de la Pomeroy, were given special commission as 'knights of the king's private household' to report of anyone spreading rumors of the king's death.[2]

The following year, the king made peace with the Church, ending the feud on the feast of the Ascension, the only concession being that he symbolically gave the Pope the kingdom so that he could rent it back every year (this, the English Treasury continued paying for another century and a half). The six-year interdict had been hugely profitable for John, and after it was over he agreed that compensation should be paid to all the dioceses he had drained of money. However, he fixed the sum at an absurdly low level and then paid up only a third of the amount.

After years of rinsing the Church of money, John was the richest King of England who ever lived; he celebrated his fourteenth year of rule that autumn by putting Peter of Wakefield and his son to death, the amateur mystic being torn apart between horses (it's fair to say John could be prickly about criticism).

And so, richer than ever and master of Britain, at the end of 1213 John went to meet some of the rebel barons, who had become known as the Northerners, a supposedly conciliatory gesture although part of the aim of bringing his whole entourage was to show his might. On November 1, he met them at Wallingford in Oxfordshire where he made promises about upholding liberties, promises that he clearly had no intention of keeping. A week later, he called all the barons to come to Oxford unarmed, while his knights turned up with weapons. It was a sort of thirteenth-century equivalent of a Bond villain throwing his killer shark a lump of meat in front of his guests.

It was not an accident that the barons' rebellion would begin in the north, as the king had been especially rapacious in this distinctive region. English kings tended to avoid the north if possible, which was even more dangerous than the rest of the country and whose politics were tied up with ancient feuds. It was a land full of tough, resolute people like Ughtred Smith of Buteland in Northumbria, who in 1249 casually pulled an arrow out of his head on the way home, 'so that my wife may not see it, for she would perhaps grieve over much.'[3] The Lionheart never went north once, getting as far as Nottingham, which was enough for him. John, however, visited the region four times in the first five years of his reign, and always to raise money; on his 1199–1200 tour around England he raised £41,000 in fines, mostly in the north. During his 1201 visit, he fined the citizens of York £100 for failing to welcome him with sufficient honor. On that same trip he also went digging for buried treasure in Corbridge in Northumberland, without luck—it can't have been very reassuring to see the man in charge of the treasury reduced to such desperado behavior.

With all this money, John had also managed to build a pretty good navy—the one thing John did do quite well, which may have been due to his youthful experience of running parts of the country on either side of the Irish Sea. (In addition, it was the case that, when the king of England also controlled Normandy, there was no need for a navy.) So between 1209 and 1212, for example, twenty new galleys and thirty transporters and other ships were launched at the king's expense. In fact, England's great adventure as a maritime power really began with John, and in particular in May 1213, at Damme in Flanders, when the English destroyed the French fleet, the first significant naval battle in English history. But even this victory was spectacularly unheroic; John's naval force had turned up and found the entire French fleet at anchor, some 1,700 ships almost completely unattended. The English simply burned them down, stole all the treasure, and headed home—a clear, if not entirely noble victory.

Once again, the king decided to invade France, building an alliance with his nephew Otto the emperor of Germany and the rulers of Flanders and Saxony. The scheme, which in terms of relative financial expenditure rivaled that of 1066 or the Normandy Invasion of 1944[4] was a massive enterprise, yet it all went terribly wrong. In July 1213, John assembled his fleet in Portsmouth, but just as in 1205, the barons refused to come with him and he 'showed his disgust by putting to sea with his household and cruising as far as Jersey. From this futile expedition he returned within three days to take his vengeance on the barons who had thwarted him.'[5]

Undeterred, he vowed to invade again and to raise money. In January 1214, John auctioned off his first wife to the baron Geoffrey de Mandeville for 20,000 marks, which Geoffrey couldn't afford, and since she was too old to have kids, he probably did not want her. The amount of money was enormous, the equivalent of tens of millions of dollars today, and Geoffrey was already not a fan of John as his first wife had been Fiztwalter's daughter. But if Geoffrey did not go ahead with the marriage, John threatened him with a loss of his whole inheritance. De Mandeville would end up joining the rebels, not surprisingly.

The following month, February 1214, John arrived in La Rochelle on the west coast of France but retreated when the king of France's son Louis threatened to attack, even though John had a much bigger force. John liked battles he could easily win, as in against enfeebled Welsh chieftains, but whenever there was any trouble, he fled. As the troubadour Bertran de Born sang: 'No man may ever trust him, for his heart is soft and cowardly.' It was this behavior that led to the great disaster at Bouvines.

The army in France was led by the king's half brother, William Longsword, one of Henry II's numerous bastards, who, in the beginning, did well in Flanders. (It says something about the old king's rapacious sexual appetites that Longsword's mother, the countess of Norfolk, was the cousin of another of Henry II's mistresses and the daughter of yet another.) But things soon went badly. John had formed alliances with the rulers of Toulouse and Aragon, but the latter was soon killed and the former exiled. Otto the Emperor, John's other ally, was then caught unawares by the French and the enterprise culminated with the disaster at Bouvines in July 1214, when John's last hope of holding onto his continental empire faded. Longsword had advised against fighting at Bouvines, but the English army charged straight at the French—and were massacred. John's grand alliance had failed, and pretty much ten years' worth of money went up in smoke; Longsword was captured and while he was in a French jail, John tried to have sex with his wife. When the battle was happening, John was four hundred miles away in La Rochelle, unaware what was going on.

And so when John returned from France in October 1214, he was broke and his opponents were now swelling in number.

Although John made more concessions to the Church, Archbishop Langton was also sympathetic to the rebels; at some point he adopted as his emblem a symbol of St. Thomas Becket, a none-too-subtle hint at where his heart lay. Langton was a great scholar, who wrote page upon page of totally impenetrable commentary on the Bible. However, there was a theme in his later writing, much of which seemed to focus on the bad kings of the Old Testament who broke God's law and who therefore had terrible things done to them. Biblical kings, he wrote, had a book of laws written down by the priests; today's kings though ignore the advice of priests and rule without restraint. The archbishop gave lectures in which he attacked these modern rulers who tax not out of necessity but greed and vanity, and where he said kingship was a punishment to mankind. He also attacked 'princes who flee from lengthy sermons.' Who could he have been referring to?

John did have some clerics on side: in his absence during his clumsy invasion, John appointed one of the least popular ministers, Peter des Roches, Bishop of Winchester, to run things. Des Roches had won the king's favor by backing him against Langton; the bishop was 'slack at scripture, sharp at accounting,' according to one not very sympathetic account.

Archbishop Langton was perhaps intellectually the most important figure behind Magna Carta, and although he may have not have written it (no one knows exactly who did, although it was certainly a collaboration), he played a big part in suggesting the idea; in 1213, he had raised the subject of Henry I's coronation charter, which had never been thought of before.

Strangely, one Sir Roger de Estreby of Lincolnshire, who was a mixture of inspired forward thinker and raving lunatic, had raised the idea of a charter of sorts in 1179. Sir Roger had petitioned Henry II to implement a seven-point program under which no one could be put to death without fair trial, that everyone should be allowed to come into their inheritance, and that positions should not be acquired by bribery. In some ways, he was a sort of mad prophet of democracy before his time, although he did say the entire program had been laid out to him in a vision by the Archangel Gabriel and St. Peter, and one of his more controversial ideas was that all Jews should be driven out of England after first being fleeced of all their money.

In July 1213, the king swore to uphold the laws of Edward the Confessor, a promise made by every king since Henry I and duly ignored (and whether Edward's time was that great is another matter). That month, Langton and some barons met the king's ministers at St. Albans and the following year at Bury St. Edmunds (both towns have, down the years, claimed to be the home of Magna Carta).

At some point, the barons began writing what became known as the Unknown Charter, which turned up in the French national archives in 1890, a sheet of parchment that included a copy of Henry I's coronation charter, plus about a dozen additional clauses that must have been thought up between 1213 and June 1215. It begins: 'King John concedes that he will arrest no man without judgement nor accept any payment for justice nor commit any unjust act,' a line of writing that clearly evolved into Clauses 39 and 40. Some early clauses were dropped, mainly referring to forced service abroad, which was no longer applicable in 1215 when the war was lost.

In January 1215, in a last desperate bid to distract from his troubles at home, John announced he was going on crusade, and that anyone who followed him would get to wear a shiny white cross. There were no takers, however, and the barons thought this pledge was done to 'defraud them of their proposals.' However, having taken the cross, or at least having promised to, the king was immune from attack (one of the reasons John had found it so difficult to find allies against his brother). From now on he took to wearing a white cross on his lapel.

That month, the king and forty barons met in London, agreeing to rendezvous again in April. The rebels, led by Fitzwalter, demanded that the king obey Henry I's Charter of Liberties, but

John stalled and then double-crossed them, asking the Pope to intervene. The Holy Father would obviously support the king; not only was the Holy See naturally sympathetic to the monarch—John had also handed over the kingdom to them—but under Canon Law, no settlement made under duress was binding, and since kings were unlikely to make concessions in other circumstances, that was that, then.

The Northerners raised an army and headed south. Fitzwalter was in charge when at Brackley, Northamptonshire, on May 5, 1215, a group of barons officially renounced their loyalty to the king, who had failed to show up for a meeting. (Brackley, along with Blyth, Salisbury, Stamford, and Warwick, was one of the official tournament venues installed by Richard, and it was at tournaments that conspiracies were usually hatched.)

Diffidation, the process of renouncing fealty, was an extremely dangerous business, and one risked not just execution but having the entire family estate taken away.

Fitzwalter, who was obviously a shy, retiring fellow, declared himself Marshal of the Army of God and the Holy Church. Among the other Northerners were Richard de Percy, an early member of the powerful Northumberland family who would feature prominently in the next couple of centuries; Roger de Montbegon of Lancashire; and William de Mowbray, a Yorkshire baron who was said to be 'most valiant' but 'as small as a dwarf.' Another, French-born, William de Forz, who was in his early twenties, joined because his mother Hawisa had to pay 5,000 marks to avoid being forcibly remarried. And although William Marshal had remained loyal to the king, his eldest son William Marshal the Younger was among the rebels, many of whom were young.

Then there was Bishop Giles de Briouze, son of Matilda: in March, John had restored him to his position after his previous trouble with the family, only then to make a fresh demand of 9,000 marks. But the fact that John had already starved his brother and mother to death must have been something of a sore point for Giles beforehand. He joined the opposition in April, the only churchman to be officially part of the rebellion. Also on board were Robert de Ros and John de Lacy; Robert had had to offer 2,000 marks 'to have his lands and his castle of which he was disseised because of the benevolence of the king' (benevolence then means the opposite of what it means now). John had made de Lacy pay 7,000 marks and left him hanging in debt for two years, even after he had come to France with him. Eventually he had had enough.

The barons had begun besieging the royal castle at Northampton, but they showed themselves to be quite useless and it went embarrassingly badly, with Fitzwalter's standard-bearer 'pierced through the head with a bolt from a crossbow.' Fitzwalter, despite his grand personal seal that showed him as a terrifying warrior on horseback, and his notorious temper and personal violence, was not the greatest of military commanders. He was held responsible for a major defeat at Vaudreuil in 1202, becoming an object 'of ridicule and contempt.'

On May 12, the king ordered that the rebel barons' castles be seized, but five days later there was an effective coup in London and the Northerners controlled the city. At this point, the king was persuaded he had to meet with Archbishop Langton, who was instrumental in bringing the monarch and the major barons together in June on the road between Windsor and London. The spot of Runnymede was chosen because it was impossible to ambush anyone at that location, the ground being too marshy for battle. There, on June 10, the rebels drew up a list of demands called 'the Articles of the Barons' in the hope of averting a civil war; these would be very similar to Magna Carta, especially its most important clauses, 39 and 40.

What followed was not that unusual—almost every English king until the eighteenth century experienced rebellion of some sort—except that this time the rebels did something quite radical, forcing the monarch to issue a charter by which he and his successors would be restricted by law.

When Marshal and Langton relayed to King John the demands at Brackley, he flew into a rage. 'Why, amongst these unjust demands, did not the barons ask for my kingdom also?' Matthew Paris wrote in private that John 'gnashed his teeth, rolled his eyes, grabbed sticks and straws and gnawed them like a madman' while all these negotiations were going on.

On June 10, John had dinner in Windsor Castle with Abbot Hugh of Bury St. Edmunds. One of the abbot's friends made an innocuous remark that somehow annoyed John, and he flew into a rage and shouted at him until the man became 'amazingly red' and fled.

On the fourteenth, John went to church. The lesson was a reading of the fourth chapter of the Revelation of St. John. It was about twenty-four elders wearing crowns 'bowed before an enthroned, divine being the color of deep red gemstones, whose throne was surrounded by a rainbow that shimmered.' It concludes with the elders 'bowing before their master's throne and throwing away their crowns.' Whether this was a good or bad omen is hard to tell. The following day the most famous document in legal history would be made.

CHAPTER TWELVE

No Freeman Shall Be Arrested

Charters were not new. As well as those that had been pledged by Ethelred the Unready and Henry I, Simon de Montfort had three years earlier issued a similar charter in his southern French territories, called the Statute of Pamiers (after he had massacred much of the population). Although the Northerners clearly did not have any sort of democracy in mind, the aim of the agreement was bold—addressing not just one bad king but also the very situation that allowed kings to get away with misruling.

But in retrospect, unlike, say, the American Constitution, which had been clearly influenced by it, Magna Carta looks like a mixed bunch of ideas and demands, some timeless and others odd, petty or actually malicious. Clause 33, for instance—'Henceforth all fish-weirs will be completely removed from the Thames and the Medway'—is not something an Englishman would get misty-eyed about, or often would have heard quoted in legal dramas, but at the time it was considered very important; fish-weirs (which are used to catch the animals) can mess up the navigation of rivers, and at a time when the average calorie intake was 1,500 a day, fishing was not just a pastime.[1]

Other provisions dealt with practical and mundane things such as the standardization of weights and measures, or who was obliged to build bridges and control the corn supply. Clause 23, ordering the building of bridges, was included largely to help make hunting with falcons easier, which says something about the concerns of those who drew up Magna Carta.

But John's misrule is clear in most of the document, such as in Clause 50, which dealt with his French cronies: 'We shall dismiss completely from their offices the relations of Girard d'Athée . . . namely Engelard de Cigogné, Peter, Guy and Andrew de Chanceaux, Guy de Cigogné, Geoffrey de Martigny with his brothers [and] Philip Mark, the Sheriff of Nottingham.' Then there was Clause 51, promising the expulsion of all 'alien knights, crossbowmen, serjeants and mercenaries who have come with horses and arms to the injury of the realm,' which was running along the same lines.

Forest laws were also a huge gripe, with forest fines accounting for half of all state revenue; Clause 53 sought to deal with this, giving 'respeite,' although it states that this and other issues relating to his brother's and father's reigns should only be resolved when John returned from crusade (John clearly had no intention of going on crusade, which any sane person knew by that point was a grueling task with a high risk of death). Another five of the clauses dealt with reducing the power of the sheriffs.

Many more clauses concern money, and the king's attempts to extract it from the barons. As with Henry I's charter, there were aspects concerning widows; Clause 8 protected them from disparagement, which meant a marriage to someone of a lower status, stating that 'no widow shall be compelled to marry'; Clauses 6 and 7 were also about marriage, while debt took up clauses 9-11 and 26-27.

London was rewarded for its support with Clause 13, ensuring the city's freedom of trade, and only one commoner witnessed the signing of Magna Carta, London Lord Mayor William Hardel. The people of London also wanted more self-government, as was increasingly becoming common for cities across western Europe (Bayonne in Gascony had become the latest to receive its own charter in April 1215). In 1191, London had also had its first elected Lord Mayor, the oddly named Henry Fitz-Ailwin de Londonestone (appropriately, his main act as mayor was encouraging the use of stone, a case of nominative determinism if ever there was one).[2] John, however, removed a clause from the draft Articles of the Barons giving rights to Londoners to seek consent about taxes imposed on them, one interpretation being that he resented the upstart London merchants making demands on the king, it being bad enough when fellow nobles did so.

Londoners were concerned with trade—which had been affected by the recent conflict—and as always with trying to make as much money as possible, hence the rather progressive Clause 41, which stated that no foreign merchants were to be harassed, except when their countries were at war with England. And even then 'until we . . . know how the merchants of our land are treated in the enemy country; and if ours are safe there, the others shall be safe in our land.'

There were also benefits for merchants and even villeins, the lowest form of life in medieval England; the Crown couldn't snatch them, perhaps only because this would financially harm their lord. However, it was purposefully un-egalitarian, for Clause 20 protected villeines only from amercements imposed by the king. Lords could still do whatever they liked.

Peasants were more concerned about something that appeared in the Unknown Charter but was left out of the 1215 agreement: that 'no man should lose life or limb' for offenses against animals in the forest. Neither is there anything in Magna Carta 'to deal with the malpractices of Lords,' as in the earlier document. (Otherwise, fifty-six of Magna Carta's sixty-three clauses were also found in the Articles of the Barons.)

We could get carried away with the idea it was progressive by later standards. Clause 54, for example, states 'no man shall be arrested or imprisoned because of the appeal of a woman for the death of anyone but her husband.' Clauses 10 and 11 are about debts owed to Jews, although it shouldn't necessarily be seen as hostility toward Jews in themselves. In the Borat-esque nightmare world that was thirteenth-century England, Jews were effectively owned by the king who would take over any debts owed to them, so the animus here was directed at the monarch, rather than the Jews in particular. (That being said, both sides attacked Jews when they had the opportunity.) John's son Henry would later sell the Jewish community to his brother Richard in 1255 for 5,000 marks.

But the document was groundbreaking, nonetheless, and Clause 1 ends with the solemn assurance '. . . we have granted to all the freemen of our realm for ourselves and our heirs for ever all the liberties written below, to have and to hold, them and their heirs from us and our heirs.' For a king to grant *in perpetuum* the rights of freemen was a momentous step.

The most important clauses, however, were 38–40, which deal with arbitrary accusations and the idea of justice.

Clause 38 stated that 'no bailiff is in future to put anyone to law by his accusation alone, without trustworthy witnesses being brought forward.' In other words, people could not be sentenced without credible witnesses.

Then comes the most important sentence in legal history, Clause 39: 'No freeman shall be arrested or imprisoned or dispossessed or outlawed or banished or in any way molested, nor will we go upon him nor send upon him, except by the lawful judgment of his peers and the law of the land.' Clause 40 states a similar theme that 'To no one will we sell, to no one will we deny or delay, right or justice.'

Clause 39 and Clause 40 are still the law in England, although confusingly they are also both called Clause 29, as the 1297 reissue of the charter edited it down. Together, Clauses 38–40 form the backbone of English liberties, influencing the concept of due legal process and equality before the law. Those ideas have spread way beyond this half island and, largely thanks to the United States's global domination, are seen as almost universal rights.

For that we have to thank Fitzwalter, a man who himself had been declared an outlaw without a trial and so demanded that it should never happen again. This would have a huge effect on what we now regard as human rights in the twenty-first century; whether Fitzwalter would fit in at a dinner party of progressive lawyers in New York or London today is besides the point.

Still, as much as Clauses 38–40 have become almost sacred to English history, they may have been copied from the Germans; back in the eleventh century, the Emperor Conrad II had protected knights from arbitrary seizures except 'save according to the constitution of our ancestors and the judgment of their peers.'[3]

Most grating to the king, though, was the Security Clause, 61, which ensured that twenty-five barons would oversee the agreement and keep an eye on the king. Under the barons' proposal, any four of the twenty-five could confront the king, and if he failed to act on these complaints, all twenty-five should seize his castles, lands, and possessions. The twenty-five were able to act if the king or his minister offended 'anyone in anything,' and it also suggested that people take an oath to the group. Clause 61 was therefore hugely provocative, stating the twenty-five were empowered to 'assail [the king] in every way possible' if he broke the treaty. This would effectively mean a permanent check and balance on royal power, something that a half-mad paranoid drunk like John was hardly going to be keen on. Later, his own mercenaries made fun of him saying there were 'twenty-five kings of England.'

The number twenty-five may have had some biblical meaning, according to some theories, being the square of five, the number of the law according to St. Augustine (five books are in the Pentateuch, Moses's law). Or it might have just been a convenient number (the current British cabinet is of similar size).

John was a bad king, but the charter was aimed at the dynasty as a whole. Ralph of Coggeshall, writing soon after, said Magna Carta was to end 'the evil customs which the father and brother of the king had created to the detriment of the Church and kingdom, along with those abuses which the king had added.'

The charter was agreed upon, and on June 15 it was engrossed, the medieval term for the drawing up of legal documents; John would not have actually signed it, although nineteenth-century drawings in children's history books always show the king doing so, often with, a stern-looking baron pointing at a piece of paper as if to say 'sign here, pal.' Some forty copies were made—the 3,500-word document of the 'Greater Charter' taking eight hours to write—and distributed across the country.

A deadline was therefore set for August 15 for the conditions on both sides to be fulfilled, at which point the rebels would hand over London. Naturally, John never went through with his promises, and probably didn't have the slightest intention of ever doing so.

John double-crosses the barons, obviously

John put off sacking his continental henchmen, as demanded, while the barons refused to hand over the Tower of London, and so the country slid into war. Among those who joined the rebels, opening up Marlborough Castle to them, was John's sidekick Hugh de Neville, who'd presumably had enough of the king and his great japes. Afterwards, John claimed that the treaty was made under duress, and so not binding. Just as he hoped, the Church refused to recognize Magna Carta because of Canon Law, and on August 24, Pope Innocent excommunicated thirty barons for rebellion, as well as the entire population of London, calling the charter shameful and unjust, and saying it 'dishonors the Apostolic See, injures the king's rights and shames the English nation' declaring it 'null and void.' Innocent III said the rebel barons were 'worse than Saracens.'

The news of the excommunications arrived in England on September 17 and the king ordered the seizing of rebel lands, the most important being Rochester Castle, the key to control of London, which with a tower 125 feet in height was at the time the tallest building in Europe.

The castle had been given to Stephen Langton as part of the peace treaty, but soon afterwards the rebels had turned up. The king now told Archbishop Langton to hand it over, but Langton replied in the language of Magna Carta, demanding the proper judgment before his peers. John wasn't interested in any of that by now and began to besiege the castle on October 13, officially starting the civil war known as the First Barons War.

Langton, a neutral figure who was mistrusted by both king and barons, refused to publish the Pope's excommunications and was therefore suspended. He left the country, having tried and failed to bring the two sides to their senses.

John now ordered forty pigs to be sent to Rochester Castle, 'the sort least good for eating,' and had a tunnel dug underneath one of its towers; he then had all the pig fat poured in the tunnel and set it alight. At this point, John wasn't acting very reasonably—again, think Alan Rickman in *Prince of Thieves*. It must have been quite an event; the garrison defending the castle were starving by now and reduced to eating their mangy horses. The first thing they would have noticed was the scent of wood smoke mixed with bacon—then the castle's towers came down as the huge fat-fire did its work.

But while the castle was being defended by just one nobleman, William of Aubigny (a former favorite of John), the barons in London couldn't be bothered to come to his aid, instead spending their time 'gambling at dice, drinking the best wines, which were freely available, and indulging in all the other vices.'[4] Rochester was starved into surrender in November; John wanted the entire garrison put to death but was persuaded otherwise by one of his lieutenants.

It's true to say that while John was acting like a pantomime villain, the barons weren't great people either. After Magna Carta was agreed upon, they had made further demands, including the replacement of des Roches, while John had, in fairness, already begun restoring lands, as per Clause 52, including those of Fitzwalter and de Vesci who was allowed to run his dogs in the forest of Northumberland 'as he ought to have this and is accustomed.' As one historian describes: 'Once in power [the barons] revealed the pettiness and arrogance common in men placed in positions beyond their capacity or their deserts. They broke faith at once by refusing to fulfill their promises to the king.'[5]

The rebels now wrote to King Philip of France calling for his help, and his twenty-eight-year-old son Prince Louis duly invaded, claiming the throne through his wife Blanche, Henry II's granddaughter. For a while, a French army actually occupied London, while John controlled only the southwest of England. De Vesci was on his way to do homage to Louis when he was killed with an arrow shot through his brain. Alongside him that day was King Alexander II of Scotland, who now joined the rebels, invading Northumberland, 'the debatable lands' as these border regions were known in medieval times because they changed hands so often.

John, in response, arrived in Berwick in January 1216, burning down the city when he could not get hold of the Scottish king, and apparently saying he would 'run the little sandy fox-cub to earth.' He headed back and by March he controlled most of southern and eastern England.

Along the way, the king didn't make any friends. Roger of Wendover (admittedly one of John's enemies) reported: 'Sword in hand they ransacked towns, houses, cemeteries, churches. Even priests at the altar were seized, tortured and robbed. Knights and others were hung up by their feet and legs or by their hands, fingers and thumbs, salt and vinegar were thrown in their eyes; others were roasted over burning coals and then dropped into cold water.'

Over the winter of 1215–1216, John's men went on the rampage, 'running about with drawn swords and open knives,' ransacking and robbing. John was torturing captives, while the royalist army was described as 'the limbs of the devil' and likened to a plague of locusts who 'ravaged the whole country with fire and sword.' The king had always surrounded himself with villainous sidekicks, but the characters of his final years were the worst, among them his military commander Faulkes of Breaute, called the 'scourge of the earth' and a 'most evil robber.'

With the winter of 1216 approaching it looked like the king had the upper hand, militarily, even though two-thirds of England's aristocracy had formally renounced him. His half brother William Longspree even joined the rebels in May 1216, and only Marshal, with his 'I was only obeying orders' mind-set of unswerving devotion to authority, remained loyal to the end.

John had succeeded in recapturing much of southern England when he got dysentery in King's Lynn, and then while trying to get to safer territory in Nottinghamshire he lost the crown jewels in the Wash. When he arrived in Newark, he treated the potentially fatal illness with nature's best medicine: booze. Drink yourself through it, as they say. The king's 'pernicious gluttony' led him, as Wendover said, to 'surfeit himself with peaches and drinking new cider, which greatly increased and aggravated the fever.'

The king passed away at midnight during a whirlwind, finally killed by his gluttony 'for he could never fill his belly full enough to satisfy him.'[6] Ralph of Coggeshall, a Cistercian, and so probably somewhat hostile, recorded that when John died, townspeople saw 'many horrible and fantastic visions . . . the tenor of which we will forgo describing here,' but the gist of Ralph's message was that these were the horrors and torments John was suffering in hell.*

In perhaps his only kind gesture, and aware that now was not a good time to be making enemies, John had allowed the sister of Matilda de Briouze to found a religious house to pray for the Lady of Hay and her son. In a letter on October 15, days before his death, John had written to the Pope suggesting 'He who punishes beyond deserts and rewards beyond deserts, will look on us with the eye of his mercy, and deem us worthy to be placed in the number of the elect.' As Magna Carta historian David Carpenter put it: 'some hope, one might think.'

John died unloved, and as the monk Matthew Paris famously put it: 'Hell herself felt defiled by his admission.' He was buried at Worcester Cathedral, although the actual whereabouts of his body soon became a mystery, and everyone assumed it was lost until his coffin was discovered in 1797. The corpse was partly putrefied, and 'a vast quantity of the dry skins of maggots were dispersed over the body.' Rather than a crown on his head, as was the norm for medieval kings, they found a monk's cowl, the thinking being it had been placed there to aid his journey to heaven—which was probably a bit on the optimistic side.

Much of his body was stolen by souvenir hunters, although his thumb bone was recovered, and the composer Edward Elgar bought his sandals and stockings and donated them to the cathedral, where they remain today.[7]

John's rule had been a miserable failure. He had made the crucial mistake of alienating the powerful; he was fond of poking fun at any pomposity, which could make him almost seem like a decent man-of-the-people type, if you can overlook the numerous murders.

---

*   This was a bit of a theme: Osbert fitzHervey, one of John's cronies, was pictured by Ralph in hell being 'forced to swallow and then regurgitate burning coins.'

And his personal habits, though strange to his fellows, would make him far more suited to the twenty-first century. He was the first king since classical times to sport a dressing gown, and he shocked court society by regularly taking baths, sometimes once a month, when many people took as many in a lifetime; although most historians are now doubtful of contemporary accounts of him spending the whole morning in bed reading.[8] The one good thing he did do was found a city on the River Mersey in 1207 called Liverpool, so inadvertently we can thank him for the Beatles.

But history can be a funny thing; as Winston Churchill put it in *The History of the English-Speaking Peoples*, 'When the long tally is added, it will be seen that the British nation and the English-speaking world owe far more to the vices of John than to the labors of virtuous sovereigns; for it was through the union of many forces against him that the most famous milestone of our rights and freedom was in fact set up.'

CHAPTER THIRTEEN

Parliament

Had John not died when he did, it's likely that Magna Carta would have gone down as just another empty promise kings are forced to make from time to time. But as it was, his son Henry was just nine years old and had to contend with a Frenchman running around calling himself king. To win back the barons, the new regime was therefore forced to make permanent concessions.

Before he died, John had appointed William Marshal as regent, and now seventy he led the battle against the invaders and promised to carry the boy king 'on his shoulders' from island to island if need be, an emotional scene in which the child was apparently in tears. King Henry III was crowned by a small group of courtiers in Gloucester, but London was controlled by the rebels and the French, and throughout history whoever controls London controls England. To cap John's loser legacy, Henry III was crowned with his mother's bracelet as his father had lost or perhaps sold the crown, like a deadbeat dad. And to make matters worse, Henry's coronation banquet was disturbed by news that Marshal's nearby castle of Goodrich was under attack.

Louis controlled over half the kingdom and had, in May 1216, received a triumphant welcome in the capital. However, the friendliness wouldn't last and the French soon became unpopular; they had brought with them a supply of their national drink, but since then had 'done nothing except drink all the wine in the city and then complain about the ale.'[1]

In desperation, the guardians of the new monarch therefore reissued the charter at Bristol in November 1216. Some bits were removed, such as the Security Clause, and the part about the king's aliens, but the rest of it was authorized by the Crown, giving the document much greater authenticity. It was signed by Marshal and the papal legate Guala Bicchieri. At this point, many of the aristocrats opposed to John, among them the younger William Marshal, pledged loyalty to his son, and these *reversi*, or returners, helped to save the royal family.

And at Lincoln in May 1217, Crown forces beat the French, the loyalists led by the geriatric but still enthusiastic Marshal, now fighting alongside his son. Before the battle, Marshal gave a rousing patriotic speech, telling everyone they had a 'chance to free our land,' to seek 'eternal glory' in victory, and feel no fear as they would soon be 'in paradise.' He concluded: 'God knows who are his loyal servants, of that I am completely certain' while the French would be sent 'down to hell.'

Henry's army then won a naval battle off the coast of Kent, even though Louis's ships were reinforced by a French fleet led by Eustace the Monk, an adventurer turned pirate who was also the subject of a popular romantic-ish poem. Eustace Busquet was the son of a nobleman who had left the Church to become a sword for hire and had worked for King John before changing sides. Now on August 24, 1217, at the Battle of Sandwich, came the conclusive confrontation; Marshal was on the front line during the encounter, in which four thousand were killed, with pots of lime powder thrown on to enemy decks. Eustace was found cowering below decks, dragged into the light, and beheaded.

Afterwards Louis went into negotiations. Seeing how his predecessor went out, he could not have been that desperate to do the job, because the ruling regents in London simply bribed him to leave with 10,000 marks, or a quarter of the country's annual revenue, to where he 'departed to besiege smaller castles,' as Roger of Wendover sarcastically put it. He still got to be King of France when he was older, though.

From a position of strength, the government reissued the charter once again in November 1217, alongside another charter, one that dealt with the forests. To distinguish between the two, the former became known as the Great Charter, or Magna Carta. Peter des Roches, John's old buddy and the villain of the piece, tried to overturn Magna Carta for the next twenty years but the genie was out of the bottle.

However, the war between the king and the barons did not end there, and it would be another fifty years before the conflict was resolved. The new king's long reign—not beaten until the insane George III in 1816—would serve as a continuation of the struggle between Crown and nobles, called the Second Barons' War. This would end with a final settlement at the end of the century in which the barons notionally lost (their leader had his testicles cut off and hung around his nose which suggests he certainly didn't triumph) but in a sense they won by establishing Magna Carta and a new innovation of Henry III's reign, the Parliament.

In contrast to his atheistic father, the new king went to Mass five times a day and was so holy that when he visited Paris, the King of France got so fed up waiting for him to arrive he banned priests from going near him in case he'd insist on yet another Mass. Whereas John was a monster, Henry was a somewhat gentle figure who loved religion and art and did much to enrich the culture of the country. He was, however, somewhat witless, scared of thunder, and droopy eyed and, most importantly, hopeless with money.

A jester once compared Henry to Christ. Flattered, the king asked why, and was told 'Because Our Lord was as wise at the moment of His conception as when He was thirty years old; so likewise our king is as wise now as when he was a little child.' But at least he wasn't as bad as his father, who would have had the jester's eyes and tongue pulled out. Contemporaries described him as *simplex*, simple, and he was also astoundingly lazy.

Henry III was strongly influenced by the flowering of what is now called 'Gothic' medieval culture, centered on Paris, although the word Gothic was only applied much later. Henry built many churches and cathedrals that stand today, most notably Westminster Abbey (the original had become dilapidated over the years) and Canterbury Cathedral. Henry developed an obsession with the Abbey's original patron, Edward the Confessor, and had an enormous portrait of the former king painted in his bedroom. He even named his eldest son Edward.

As well as great cathedrals, Henry III's reign also saw the first zoo in London, at the Tower, where a leopard donated by the Holy Roman Emperor lived with a polar bear and a presumably rather nervous porcupine. This was the first such royal menagerie to be open to the public, the entrance fee being a dog or cat for the lion to eat.[2] In 1255, the king of France presented an elephant to Henry to add to this collection, and it was fed on beef and wine, although unfortunately two years later it drank itself to death.[3]

Alas, Marshal died in 1219, ending a life that became the embodiment of chivalry; in fact, most of the clichés about medieval knighthood come from Marshal's biography, which turned up in a jumble sale in the nineteenth century quite by chance, the most recent being the film *A Knight's Tale*, which features stories from his life. One of Marshal's last acts was to distribute his eighty fine scarlet robes to his men, the sort of largesse that was expected of a good lord; this was despite a priest telling him to sell them 'to deliver you from your sins' (i.e., give to the Church), to which Marshal replied

'Hold your tongue you wretch, I have had enough of your advice.' Of Marshal's five sons, all died quite young of hideous deaths; Richard was killed by his own vassals during one of the numerous aristocratic squabbles in Ireland, while another, Gilbert, was fatally wounded in a tournament.

Marshal's loss was felt keenly by the crown, and his two successors as regent had left the treasury in a desperate situation by the time the king assumed control. Henry's government was always broke, and this led it to make repeated concessions to the barons. In 1225, King Louis of France threatened to invade English Gascony, and in needing money to fight wars abroad and buy back castles at home, the Crown issued what would become the definitive Magna Carta, with Archbishop Stephen Langdon witnessing it once again; he had gotten his job back after both king and Pope died in 1216.

The barons were fearful of losing their hard-won privileges, and a crisis arose again in 1234 after the king had tried to revoke previous charters. In total, during his long reign, Henry III promised on at least a dozen occasions to uphold Magna Carta. This 1237 Magna Carta was witnessed by des Roches and Marshal's sons. By 1250, it was being proclaimed not just in Latin but in Norman French and in English; official letters sent out in 1255 in three languages confirmed it. (This also influenced the Normans, who demanded similar rights; in March 1315, Louis X of France gave them a 'Charte aux normands,' after a tax revolt.)

Failed foreign wars aggravated the Crown's problems. Henry tried to invade France in 1242, an escapade that ended in miserable failure. The conflict was begun, bizarrely, by Henry's mother, Isabella, who had left England just nine months after her son became king, having had enough of it. She had then married Hugh of Lusignan, the son of her former betrothed, despite his being engaged to her daughter Joan—'one of the most extraordinary marriages in history.'[4] Isabella started a war, setting the Poitevin barons against the King of France because she had been insulted by being told to stand when Louis's mother was seated, one of the stupider reasons for beginning a war in history; Isabella was 'killed,' as she described it when she was made to stand in the French king's chamber like some 'fatuous servant.' Then when her husband entertained the French at Lusignan, 'she ransacked the castle, took all her good[s] back to Angouleme and kept Hugh waiting outside for three days before she would see him.'[5] Hugh must have been really glad he married her.

Henry ill-advisedly became involved and returned home beaten, just like his father; his mother was lucky to escape with her life.

The king would hold meetings with the most important barons, where he'd beg for money and they'd moan about the state of the country. Henry initially tried to shift attention away from money troubles at home by embarking on Crusade, but having raised the money for the adventure, the king instead gave the cash to Pope Alexander IV, who in turn nominated Henry's son Edmund Crouchback as the King of Sicily. The throne of the island kingdom had become vacant in 1250 following the death of Frederick II, who is today perhaps most notable as a very innovative but also very cruel pioneer in the social sciences. Among his great ideas was a language deprivation experiment in which young children were raised without human interaction to see if language was natural, and another where prisoners were shut in a cask to see if their soul could be observed leaving them when they died.

Henry III seems to have been not the most hard-nosed negotiator in the world; he paid the Holy Father £90,000, almost as much as the king's ransom, for the right to the Sicilian throne—but part of the deal stated that he had to conquer it first. Henry had also signed a sub-clause that if he was defeated during the invasion, then he would be excommunicated (in fairness, Sicily has been invaded something like thirty-four times, most recently by the Allies in 1943, so he might expect to achieve this feat). Henry also promised to go on crusade which, even his best friends might tell him, would not be his thing; on the upside there would be plenty of churches to visit in the Middle East, but you had to fight your way past Muslim armies to get at them.

Pope Alexander had told Henry of 'the royal family of England whom we regard with special affection' and that in Sicily, Edmund would be 'received like the morning star.' Richard, Henry's shrewder brother, had also been offered the island but replied to the papal representative: 'You might as well try and sell me the moon as a bargain, saying "go up there and grab it."' Then the Pope double-crossed the king and gave the country to Henry's brother-in-law instead.

To the barons, this was the latest in a long line of disastrous mistakes by the king. The informal meetings had begun to take a more formalized shape, and in 1236 they were first called 'Parliament' (literally, 'a talk' in French). This Parliament met four times between 1248 and 1249, when they refused to give money to the king, complaining about corruption and the monarch's French in-laws.

And if you're a medieval monarch, the last thing you need when everything is going wrong is for God to start smiting you, and in 1258 this is exactly what He did, with a terrible famine. Some fifteen thouand are estimated to have died in London, and people visiting the capital saw rotting corpses lying in the gutter. So many inhabitants were haggard and starved that there weren't enough of them to bury the dead, which is never a good look for a city. That year, the queen was forced to flee by the Thames, where the mob spotted her and pelted her with manure, shouting 'down with the witch! Let's drown her!' Her eldest son had just carried out a bank robbery in the center of town, which had somewhat undermined support for the royals.

Curiously, the development of Parliament may have been influenced by an extreme weather event on the other side of the world: the massive eruption of Mount Rinjani in Indonesia in 1257, the greatest explosion in the last ten thousand years, cooled the earth by as much as two degrees centigrade and led to crop failure across Europe.[6]

This led to the barons meeting at Oxford that year, issuing the Provisions of Oxford, which made a series of demands, among them that each county and city should send two knights to Parliament, and that Parliament should choose half of a council to rule the land. The Provisions of this 'Mad Parliament' were issued not just in Latin and French but also, for the first time for any political document since the Battle of Hastings, in English too. The Oxford rebels demanded that King Henry 'faithfully keep and observe the charter of the liberties of England,' by which they meant Magna Carta.

Henry's consort, Queen Eleanor of Provence, was especially unpopular because she had the rights to many tolls, which Londoners didn't like paying. Henry and Eleanor had been married when he was twenty-eight and she was just twelve,* and she unfortunately came with lots of family members; certainly part of the motivation for the hostility to the royal family was naked xenophobia against her various hanger-on relatives. Although by marrying her, Henry was helping to import a cultural revival of art and literature from France and Germany, epitomized by the Gothic cathedrals of Notre Dame and Chartres, as well as literature and poetry, the people pelting her with excrement from London Bridge probably didn't see it that way.

These 'Savoyard' relatives of the Queen were notorious. Henry III even made the queen's uncle Boniface Archbishop of Canterbury, the last foreigner to have the job. Boniface was so unpopular he walked around with protective armor underneath his priestly vestment, and it was hardly surprising when he once punched a priest in the face over an ecclesiastical dispute, while Mathew Paris said he was 'noted more for his birth than his brains,' and spent half

---

*   And they were certainly sharing a bed within three years. We know this because a knife-wielding maniac had broken into the king's chamber in the night, but he was luckily in bed with his wife.

of his twenty-nine-year reign outside of the country.* Henry also made his French half-brother Aymer de Valence Bishop of Winchester, despite being a teenager.

The position of so many foreigners in the English court was exploited by the rebel leader, the not-very-English Simon De Montfort. De Montfort was the hero of the baron's revolt and of Parliamentary rule, but he was perhaps the least sympathetic character of the entire period. His father had led the exceptionally cruel and needlessly violent Albigensian crusade against Cathars in the south of France, and the younger Simon de Montfort had arrived in England at the age of twenty-two, having spent his teens persecuting religious minorities and without a word of English.

Married to the king's sister, another Eleanor, he was stupendously rich, and the tales of gargantuan feasting at his house would shame a Roman emperor. Variously described as the 'father of Parliament' by some and a greedy, opportunistic, violent maniac by others, De Montfort was both dashing and terrifying. In one especially pathetic moment the king once told him: 'I'm horribly frightened of thunder and lightning but, by God's head, I'm more frightened of you than all the thunder and lightning in the world.' One chronicler, the Dominican Thomas Stubbs, said of Simon that had he lived to be king 'he might have become a destroyer rather than a savior.' Another, Canon Thomas Wykes of Osney, said Simon was a criminal who called his fellow barons 'unreliable wretches.'

Henry had been upset by De Montfort marrying his sister. The couple fled to France, after which Simon briefly went on crusade,

---

* In 1249, during the height of the famine, Boniface had arrived at St. Bartholomew's priory where he ordered the canons to come to him. However, they were saying Mass, and refused, and so the archbishop grabbed the sub-prior, repeatedly punching him and saying, 'This is the way to deal with English traitors.'

although it's not known whether he saw any fighting. But he was possibly influenced by what he saw in Palestine, where an oligarchy of powerful barons ran the Kingdom of Jerusalem with a nominal king; this is clearly what he intended for England.

Exploiting popular xenophobia against the Provençals (being from just outside Paris, Simon and the southern French would have seen each other as foreigners, and spoken a different if vaguely comprehensible language), De Montfort proposed that Parliament should meet without the permission of the king. All the king's officials would be chosen annually, and subject to the new council of twenty-four, with fifteen picked by Parliament (i.e., De Montfort)—and he appealed to Magna Carta to justify his program. The king accused De Montfort of treason, to which he replied in the manner of an old-style gentleman looking for a fight: 'That word is a lie and were you not my sovereign it would be an ill hour for you when you dared utter it.'

Henry refused this radical proposal, and in 1260 there began the Second Barons' War. One of the major engagements took place at Lewes in 1264, where De Montfort gave a moving speech in which he said they were fighting for England, God, the Virgin Mary, the saints, and the Church. They called themselves the Army of God. De Montfort may have had God on his side, but the king had his extremely violent son 'the Lord Edward' on his, accompanied by a large number of bloodthirsty Scottish knights, who were more frightening than the Almighty on the ground. Among them was Robert the Bruce, whose grandson of the same name would centuries later share a platform with Edward in that moving historical documentary *Braveheart*. The conflict became so bitter that the royalists at Lewes flew the dragon banner 'that signaled the intention of fighting to the death, taking no prisoners,' the first sign that the code of chivalry was starting to break down.[7] Before the battle of Lewes, during the formal exchange of letters between sides, Edward told his uncle that 'from this time forth we will do our utmost to inflict injury upon your persons and possessions.'

On that day De Montfort's men got the upper hand, although it was inconclusive. Then in July, with the threat of a French invasion, De Montfort sent royal writs to each county calling for a national army. He received a very enthusiastic response, and though the invasion never came, it was clear who was in charge; even the Mayor of London told the king he would be his faithful man 'as long as you be good.'

Simon De Montfort was close to winning and at one point had both Henry and his son captive, but ultimately the Lord Edward won the war. The future Edward I, although he shared Henry's droopy eye, was in every respects the opposite of his father; monstrously violent and terrifying, he was still invading neighboring countries into his late sixties.

Edward became known as the leopard, after the then-common belief that the animal could change its spots; for he would side with whoever was winning, then stab them in the back and twist the knife. He had started off as a supporter and ally of De Montfort, and had once raised the money to pay for the Crown's affairs by pulling off an armed robbery at the Templars' bank, where the queen had pawned her jewelry. Edward and his followers had told the Templars he wanted to view his mother's jewels inside but when they let him in, he went around with iron hammers smashing the chests and taking the gems.

While imprisoned by the rebels, the prince had managed to convince his presumably rather dim jailors to let him try out one of their horses—and promptly rode off, shouting 'Lordlings I bid you good day.' And thereafter he conducted the conflict with the utmost ruthlessness, poisoning rebel negotiator William de Clare over breakfast negotiations (he woke up the next day and died from stomach pains, while his brother's hair fell out), employing a cross-dressing spy called Margoth, and turning up to battle in the enemy's colors. This was the trick he used at Evesham in 1265, which ended with De Montfort dead along with two of his sons.

The battle was followed by the execution of thirty rebel knights, and Edward cut off De Montfort's testicles and had them hung around his nose, while his torso was cut into four and his head sent to a noblewoman who had helped Edward escape captivity, as a touching little present. These cold-blooded executions were considered quite shocking: 'such was the murder of Evesham, for battle it was not.'

The king was almost killed because he was dressed in rebel colors, and had to cry pathetically: 'I am Henry of Winchester your king! Do not kill me!' His son led him away from the battlefield.

The king's goons enacted terrible revenge on their enemies around the country, and after the battle—afterwards Henry confiscated 254 estates from rebels. There followed widespread civil disorder and unrest among outlaws called the 'Disinherited,' many from noble families who had been forced to flee into the forest; it is during this period that the story of Robin Hood first emerges. Among the many atrocities, the Sheriff of Essex was accused of having plotted to release flying cockerels carrying incendiary bombs over London during 1267. In the 1260s, a brigand took over Bristol and ruled for several years, effectively setting himself up as local ruler. An army three hundred–strong marched around Norfolk causing havoc and doing whatever they pleased, and a band of fifty men, including the Abbots of Sherbourne and Middleton, raided the Countess of Lincoln's home at Kingston Lacy and took everything. The Prior of Bristol was even worse: his gang invaded an estate in Wiltshire and murdered all the men and raped the lady of the house.

Within a decade of Evesham, King Henry had granted the barons and their Parliament most of the power they'd demanded in the first place. The economy turned around, and best of all, in 1267, a huge shipment of wine from Gascony arrived in London, hugely improving morale. Henry III lived until 1272, becoming ever more senile as he devoted more time to hanging around churches.

In 1275, now Edward I, the new king formalized Parliament, allowing for the first time knights and burgesses (city men) into the Privy Council, the inner circle of advisers that was a sort of the forerunner to the Cabinet. Finally, in 1297, came the *Confirmatio Cartarum*, the Confirmation of the Charters, which formalized Magna Carta into law. The barons had effectively won, although admittedly to De Montfort it might not have looked that way at the time.

CHAPTER FOURTEEN

The Legacy of Magna Carta

Today the doors to the US Supreme Court feature eight panels showing important moments in legal history, one with an angry-looking King John facing a baron, between them being Magna Carta.[1]

The dream of 1215 did not end at Evesham, and while De Montfort had died, his legacy lived on. That's not to say he didn't have his faults; he was arrogant, vain, and may have turned out far worse than the king were he in charge. Even for the standards of the time, he was insanely anti-Semitic, and expelled all the Jews from Leicester, where he was earl (although compared to his nephew Edward he was Oskar Schindler).

But this aristocratic, French religious bigot is still a hero of English liberties nonetheless, as the man who tried to establish restrictions on the power of the monarch. Today his picture hangs outside the United States House of Representatives in remembrance of his legacy. He also has the honor of having a university and concert hall in Leicester named after him, as well as a non-league football stadium and a bridge on the northeast stretch of the A46 from Bath to Cleethorpes. Worth having your testicles chopped off for, surely.

In 1300, Edward I reconfirmed the Charter when there was further discontent among the aristocracy; the king may have been lying to everyone, but he at least established the precedent that kings were supposed to pretend to be bound by rules. Edward had tried to tax without consent once, in 1297, but had to back down after a near revolt; kings would never try again. From 1300, sheriffs were ordered to read the Great and Forest charters four times a year 'before the people in full county court' and also at Westminster Hall 'in the language of the country' as well as Latin, something which would have taken well over an hour: 'Some in the county court may have listened with rapt attention. Others probably went out to the alehouse.'[2] Back in 1279, Archbishop Peckham ordered Magna Carta to be placed in cathedrals and big churches, but Edward ordered them taken down, as he didn't like this individual initiative. It was already becoming a sacred document.

Twice, Magna Carta helped to remove rulers in the fourteenth century. In addition, Edward III was the first king effectively appointed by Parliament after his father had been overthrown in 1327. Parliament often reaffirmed the charter to the monarch, with forty such announcements by 1400.[3] Under Edward III, the so-called 'six statutes' spelled out the idea of due process, and this became perhaps the most important plank of freedom in the English-speaking world. The wording of Charter 39 was expanded, with 'free man' changed to 'no man, of whatever estate or condition he may be,' and stating that no one could be dispossessed, imprisoned, or executed without 'due process of law,' the first time that phrase was used.

Magna Carta was last issued in 1423 and was barely referenced in the later fifteenth or sixteenth centuries, with the country going through periods of dynastic fighting followed by Tudor despotism. By Elizabeth I's time, Magna Carta was so little cared about that William Shakespeare's play *King John* didn't even mention it. The work mainly attacks John for not standing up to the Pope enough, which at this time of anti-Catholic paranoia was seen as a far bigger crime than a few murders and violations of the law.

The first print edition of the Great Charter appeared, in Latin, in 1508, followed by an English translation in 1534. As the number of books published and sold rocketed in the sixteenth century, along with literacy levels, there came a new interest in the law. This period saw the growth of two conflicting ideas: firstly absolutism, which had developed out of the practical reality of monarchies becoming centralized and rulers more powerful. Its origins were in the medieval period but only took truly lunatic form in the reign of 'Sun King' Louis XIV of France from 1643, who built an enormous palace that he filled with enough rooms so that he could always face the sun, whatever time of day. His policies would cripple the economy, suppress free expression, and undermine the growth of civil society, while across the Channel, Englishmen smugly watched while stuffing their faces with roast beef.

In England, Elizabeth's incomprehensible Scottish successor James I used to lecture Parliament about his belief in the divine right of kings, yet there was also a rival idea developing—that the rights of ordinary Englishmen were natural and ancient and had only been usurped by monarchs. Magna Carta would be essential to this.

Opponents of James I and his son Charles I talked of England's 'ancient constitution,' and traced it through Magna Carta and further back to the Anglo-Saxon witans and forest councils of the Saxons in Germany. Some of this may have been a little on the romantic side, if not actual junk history, but it created precedents and rights that became self-fulfilling.

Certainly, the text to the Unknown Charter makes clear that the barons thought they were restoring law, rather than innovating, for in the words of one historian they 'believed that good law had once existed and that their duty lay in recalling and restoring it. To this extent, Magna Carta is to be viewed as a deeply conservative, not as a deliberately radical, measure.'[4]

The most influential of these constitutionalists was the jurist Edward Coke, who saw the Great Charter as reaffirmation of ancient English rights. Coke and parliamentarian John Hampden used Magna Carta as an argument for an Ancient Constitution that the Stuarts were trying to take away. They might have used some creative history along the way; Coke thought Parliament was as old as king Arthur and even dated it back to the City of Troy where the first Britons had come from.

Coke wrote of it: 'Upon this chapter, as out of a roote, many fruitful branches of the Law of England have sprung.' He used Magna Carta as the basis of the 1628 Petition of Right, the proto-constitution that Parliament forced Charles I to sign. Charles refused to budge and would eventually meet a similar end to his ancestor John.

During the buildup to the civil war, parliamentarians cited Magna Carta in their (rather spiteful) impeachments against the Earl of Stafford in 1641 and Archbishop Laud four years later, two supporters of the king who were accused of conspiring to bring about arbitrary government and undermine Parliament. Likewise, the 1641 Grand Remonstrance against the Crown looked to Magna Carta as proof of Parliamentary rights. John Lilburne, leader of the radical Leveller group, talked of 'the ground of my freedom, I build upon the Grand charter of England.' Before the war, Lilburne had been charged with printing an unlicensed book, and it was his refusal to take an incriminating oath that would lead to the US Fifth Amendment, also known as the Right to Silence. His fellow Leveller, pamphleteer Richard Overton, was dragged to jail by his head 'as if I had been a dead dog' while holding onto his copy of Magna Carta, which 'I clapped it in my arms' until it was forced out of them. 'And thus by an assault they got the great Charter of England's Liberties and Freedoms from me; which I labored to the utmost of power in me to preserve and defend, and ever to the death shall maintain.'

However, the seventeenth century also saw controversy about what Magna Carta actually meant. Some historians, with justification, argued that it essentially only defended the barons and that it was irrelevant to an uprising by the House of Commons, which didn't even exist until the reign of Edward I. And 'ancient rights' is something of a misnomer, for generally speaking, early medieval Europe was not a place where anyone had rights. Much of this Parliamentary historical idea was also a sort of anti-French fantasy in which the Normans took away the ancient rights of freeborn Englishmen who used to sit around a forest discussing the minutiae of lawmaking and perhaps cricket.

After Parliament won the war in 1649, the victors fell out and a strongman, Puritan-MP-turned-soldier Oliver Cromwell, ended up dismissing MPs, too, and when informed by a lawyer about ancient rights, he shouted, 'I care not for the Magna Farta!' Cromwell died in 1658, and two years later Charles's son Charles II would be crowned king, but after his death his brother James II was ejected and replaced by his son-in-law, the Dutchman William of Orange (in circumstances not entirely different from those of Prince Louis in 1216). Again, Magna Carta was cited as precedent and justification, leading to the 1689 Bill of Rights, the cornerstone of the (unwritten) English constitution. The Bill of Rights confirmed English freedoms such as the right to have a reasonable bail when being tried, freedom from cruel and unusual punishments, and freedom of speech, as well as preventing royal interference with the law and, money always being an issue down the years, no taxation without royal approval.

After this, Magna Carta would continue to have great appeal to political liberals. Publisher Arthur Beardmore, a friend of radical eighteenth-century politician John Wilkes, was arrested for libeling the authoritarian Scottish minister Lord Bute in 1762, and when they came to arrest him he just happened to be teaching his

son about Magna Carta; it was a contrived PR stunt, but Bute was
unpopular and Beardmore was released.

America

It was partly thanks to Coke that Magna Carta was to have even
more influence in the new world than it did in the old. Coke was
a fervent believer in English liberties, as he set out in his book *The
Excellent Privilege of Liberty and Property Being the Birth-Right of the Freeborn Subjects of England*, polemics at the time not being known for the
brevity of their titles. In America, the Puritans and other wrangling,
bickering Protestant sects would make Magna Carta central to their
beliefs; the Quaker William Penn first published it in the colonies
in 1687.

It was Coke who helped to draft the charter of the newly established Virginia Company in 1606, which set the rules of government
for the English colonies in the new world. On this continent, he
wrote, there would be 'all liberties, franchises and immunities . . . as
if they had been abiding and born within this our realm of England.'
Instructions issued in 1618 by the Virginia Company to Governor
Sir George Yeardley were called the 'Great Charter' by Virginians,
and the General Assembly of Virginia became the first such Parliament in the western hemisphere.

Similar English liberties were guaranteed in the charters of
the other colonies, among them Massachusetts, Connecticut, and
the Carolinas. When North Carolina was established, its propri-
etors authorized its governor to grant land on the same terms as the
Great Deed of Grant of Virginia, 'a species of Magna Carta.'[5] Puritan Massachusetts's first emblem showed a man with a sword in one
hand and a copy of Magna Carta in the other.[6]

Again, most of those bringing about these fundamental changes
saw themselves as preserving the past rather than being revolution-
aries; the worst criticism a Puritan could make was to call something
an 'innovation' or 'novelty.' They were simply reviving old rights,

they said, although this could just be because it is logically easier to claim to want to preserve rather than change. In fact, even Edward the Confessor, at his coronation in 1043, had sworn to uphold the law of his Viking predecessor Canute, who in turn swore to uphold the laws of King Edgar who ruled in the tenth century. Edgar probably claimed to be upholding the laws of someone even more distant before him.

The importance of Magna Carta became even greater in the debates and quarrels that followed after Britain and its colonists had kicked the French out of North America in 1763. This would lead to rebellion and independence, and the most famous slogan of the revolutionary era—'no taxation without representation'—which was following in the spirit of Clause 14: 'And for us to have common counsel of the realm for the levying of an aid.'

When the American Constitution came to be written, it was heavily influenced by the charter, and the famous Fifth Amendment borrows from Clause 39: 'No person shall be held to answer for a capital, or otherwise infamous crime, unless on a presentment or indictment of a Grand Jury . . . nor shall any person be subject for the same offence to be twice put in jeopardy of life or limb; nor shall be compelled in any criminal case to be a witness against himself, nor be deprived of life, liberty, or property, without due process of law.' Likewise, the Sixth Amendment, which states that 'the accused shall enjoy the right to a speedy and public trial, by an impartial jury of the State and district wherein the crime shall have been committed,' was based on Clause 40, and uses the exact phrase, 'lawful judgment of peers' as appears in Clause 39.

CHAPTER FIFTEEN

Magna Carta Today

The last two centuries have seen the triumph of English-speaking ideas and armies, and the influence of Magna Carta has therefore come to grow across the world. After Britain's victory in the Napoleonic War, France, envious of the successful and moderate political constitution that had defeated them, established its own charter in 1814, with the restored monarchy restrained by law. Belgium followed suit after that country was established for no reason whatsoever in 1830.

However, most of Magna Carta was taken off the statute books in the nineteenth century when the law was tidied up (there had never previously been one book of laws, and lots of archaic ones had never been repealed, while others contradicted one another; it was a mess). The process began in 1828, with the repeal of Clause 36, followed by seventeen of the thirty-seven clauses of the 1225 charter being swept away in 1863. Another five went in the 1880s, with the last repeals in 1966 when clauses 20–22, dealing with amercements owed to the king, were removed (not really a thing that could be of much concern in 1960s England).

Today just four clauses—1, 13, 39, and 40—are law, and they remain for emotional reasons as much as anything, as the rights within are guaranteed by subsequent laws. Clause 39 in particular remains one of the most important sentences in history.

As for the actual documents, today some four copies of the original forty from 1215 still exist: one at Lincoln Cathedral, another at Salisbury Cathedral, and two at the British Library in London, one severely damaged by fire. A further twenty-three copies of reissues made between 1215 and 1300 survive in a variety of locations, among them London, Oxford, Durham, Hereford, Washington, and Canberra. Also, in the British Library is Bishop Langton's copy of the Articles of the Barons, which he took to Lambeth Palace, and which had been looted just before the seventeenth century Civil War. Other Magna Cartas will probably turn up; one from 1217 was only discovered and identified as such in 1989, while a copy from 1300 was found in Sandwich, Kent, in a Victorian scrapbook in 2015. Despite being badly damaged, it is estimated to be worth fifteen million dollars.[1] You may have one in your attic.

When, in the autumn of 1939, the Lincoln copy was taken to New York to be exhibited at the World's Fair, fourteen million people went to see it—no one observing the world that year could deny that the rule of law was quite important really in the scheme of things. When war broke out, the Americans looked after it, and the British Government, desperate to win over US support against the Nazis, attempted to force Lincoln Cathedral to donate that copy to the American people, as a goodwill gift—ironically exactly the sort of coercion that Magna Carta was supposed to stop.[2]

A generation later, after the tragic assassination of John F Kennedy, the British House of Commons honored their fallen ally with a memorial at the spot where, in George VI's words, it had all begun. One acre of land at Runnymede was transferred to the people of the United States as a gift from the Queen and her government, and is still technically US soil. The Kennedy memorial features a quote from his inaugural address: 'Let every nation know, whether it wishes us well or ill, that we shall pay any price, bear any burden, meet any hardship, support any friend, or oppose any foe in order to assure the survival and success of liberty.'

Magna Carta remains such an important part of American life that when in 2007 a copy of the 1297 Confirmation was sold by billionaire Ross Perot, it secured $21.3 million at auction from David Rubenstein, the founder of a private equity firm, who announced that he intended to put it on public display: 'Today is a good day for our country,' Rubenstein said afterwards. 'This document stands the test of time.'

Indeed it has. In fact, Magna Carta has been quoted in a number of legal disputes in recent years, such as in the US Supreme Court in debates about the legality of detaining people in Guantanamo Bay. It came up in a 2003 debate in the British Courts over the Chagos Islanders, who had been moved from their home, their lawyer citing 'unlawful exile' as being contrary to the 1215 document, while it was also used this century in a case involving native fishing rights in New Zealand.

None of this is what was intended at the time. Although Franklyn D. Roosevelt said, 'the democratic aspiration is no mere recent phase in human history. . . . it is written in Magna Carta,' Churchill was closer when he wrote that the document was 'the foundation of principles and systems of government of which neither King John nor his nobles dream'd.' Whatever the mythmaking of seventeenth-century radicals, and the motives of the barons, the acceptance of Magna Carta by Crown officials after the death of King John was a crucial event that made the rule of law possible, and it led the way to the end of arbitrary government. As the twentieth-century lawyer Lord Denning put it: 'Magna Carta is the greatest constitutional document of all times—the foundation of the freedom of the individual against the arbitrary authority of the despot.'

For that we should be grateful. As far as back as 1770 there were suggestions that June 15 be made a public holiday in England, and in recent years, the subject has come up again. It could be argued that Magna Carta Day would be a national day based on the rule of law and constitutional patriotism—good ideas that have lasted the test of time.

So each June 15, wherever you are, raise a glass to the hopelessly incompetent, cowardly alcoholic king who made it all possible.

Bibliography

This is an introduction to the subject and far more can be discovered in detail from the following:

Ackroyd, Peter. *Foundation (The History of England, Volume I)*

Asbridge, Thomas. *The Greatest Knight*

Bartlett, Robert. *England Under the Norman and Angevin Kings*

Bartlett, Robert. *The Making of Europe*

Bridges, Antony. *The Crusades*

Brooke, Christopher. *The Saxons and Norman Kings*

Carpenter, David. *Magna Carta*

Castor, Helen. *She-Wolves*

Church, Stephen. *King John*

Danziger, Danny, and Gillingham, John. *1215: The Year of Magna Carta*

Fraser, Antonia. *The Lives of the Kings and Queens of England*

Gillingham, John. *Conquest, Catastrophe and Recovery*

Gillingham, John. *Richard I*

Gimson, Andrew, *Gimson's Kings and Queens*

Hannam, James. *God's Philosophers*

Hannan, Daniel. *How We Invented Freedom*

Harvey, John. *The Plantagenets*

Hibbert, Christopher. *The English: A Social History*

Hindley, Geoffrey. *A Brief History of Magna Carta*

Jones, Dan. *Plantagenets*

Jones, Dan. *Realm Divided*

Lacey, Robert. *Great Tales from English History*

Morris, Marc. *A Great and Terrible King*

Morris, Marc. *King John*

McLynn, Frank. *Lionheart and Lackland*

Ormrod, W. M. *The Kings and Queens of England*

Palmer, Alan. *Kings and Queens of England*

Poole, A. L. *Domesday Book to Magna Carta*

Schama, Simon. *A History of Britain*

Seward, Desmond. *The Demon's Brood*

Tombs, Robert. *The English and Their History*

Vincent, Nicholas. *Magna Carta: A Very Short Introduction*

White, R. J. *A Short History of England*

Whittock, Martyn. *A Brief History of Life in the Middle Ages*

Wilson, Derek. *The Plantagenets*

Endnotes

Introduction

1. Duff Hart-Davis, *King's Counsellor: Abdication and War, The Diaries of Sir Alan Lascelles.*
2. Historian Ian Mortimer estimates that 90 percent of English people descend from Edward III, the great-great-grandson of King John, and on top of this millions of Europeans and North Americans—in which case there is a good chance that you do too.

Chapter 1

1. Nicholas Vincent, Magna Carta: *A Very Short Introduction.*
2. A. L. Poole, *From Domesday Book to Magna Carta.*

Chapter 2

1. Desmond Seward, *The Devil's Brood.*
2. Dan Jones, *Realm Divided.*
3. John Gillingham, *Conquest, Catastrophe and Recovery*
4. Over his reign, Henry II would cross the Channel twenty-four times, spending fourteen years in Normandy, thirteen in England, and seven in Anjou and Aquitaine. He would celebrate Christmas in twenty-four different places.
5. H. M. Thomas, *Shame, Masculinity and the Death of Thomas Becket,* quoted *in Realm Divided.*

6. Simon Schama, *A History of Britain.*
7. Helen Castor, *She-Wolves.*
8. Poole, *From Domesday to Magna Carta.*
9. Castor, *She-Wolves.*
10. Antony Bridges, *The Crusades.*
11. Andrew Gimson, *Gimson's Kings and Queens.*
12. Castor, *She-Wolves.*
13. Peter Ackroyd, *Foundation (the History of England, Volume I).*
14. Robert Tombs, *The English and Their History.* As Robert Tombs wrote, there were now eight hundred thousand oxen and four hundred thousand horses, which multiplied muscle over six or seven times; road density was higher than in twenty-first century, and average speeds wouldn't improve until the eighteenth century.
15. Tombs, *The English.*
16. Poole, *From Domesday.*

Chapter 3

1. The Sheriff of Middlesex spoke 'of fugitives and of those defooted.'
2. And it was mostly men; in one case from 1201, five men and one woman were suspected of a crime; it was ruled that 'let the males purge themselves by water under the assize, and Matilda by ordeal of iron.'
3. John Gillingham, *Conquest, Catastrophe and Recovery.*
4. Canon 18 of the Fourth Lateran Council proclaimed: 'No cleric may pronounce a sentence of death, or execute such a sentence, or be present at its execution. Neither shall anyone in juduical tests or ordeals by hot or cold water or hot iron bestow any blessing.'
5. Gillingham, *Conquest, Catastrophe and Recovery.*
6. Poole, *From Domesday.*
7. Tombs, *The English.*
8. Also sometimes translated as 'to have peace from the king's malevolence.'
9. Gillingham, *Conquest, Catastrophe and Recovery.*

10. Tombs, English.
11. Forest, strictly speaking, meant any land that was enclosed for use by the crown, not all of which was what we'd call forest. For example the whole of Essex was classified as a forest.
12. Christopher Hibbert, *The English: A Social History.*
13. "100, Greatest Britons," Wikepedia, https://en.wikipedia.org/wiki /100_Greatest_Britons.

Chapter 4

1. Martyn Whittock, *A Brief History of Life in the Middle Ages.*
2. Poole, *From Domesday.*
3. People also believed a woman couldn't conceive unless she enjoyed the occasion, which is daft, although researchers at University College Cork in 2016 concluded that women who had an orgasm were 15 percent more likely to conceive.
4. Danny Danziger and John Gillingham, 1215: *The Year of Magna Carta.*
5. Poole, *From Domesday.*
6. Danziger and Gillingham, *1215.*
7. Whittock. According to one estimate of the time, clerics made up 5.6 percent of the population in 1200, including 7,600 monks, 3,900 canons, and 5,300 friars.
8. Whittock. A study of people in York area between 1452 and 1530.
9. http://www.british-history.ac.uk/middx-sessions/vol1/pp155-189.
10. "Punishments at the Old Bailey," https://www.oldbaileyonline. org/static/Punishment.jsp#benefit-of-clergy.
11. Poole, *From Domesday.*
12. Ackroyd, *Foundation.*
13. "Consistitions of Clarendon," http://conclarendon.blogspot. co.uk/2013/01/the-most-renowned-case-concerning.html.
14. Harvey, *Plantagenets.*
15. The meeting was in October 1164, and Becket supposedly carried it to show he had divine protection.

16. Gimson, *Gimson's Kings and Queens.*

17. Ackroyd, *Foundation.*

Chapter 5

1. Thomas Asbridge, *The Greatest Knight.*

2. Asbridge, *Knight.*

3. Harvey, *Plantagenets.*

4. Believers point out that whatever the unlikelihood of the tale, a local flower, the Glastonbury Thorn has been proven to originate in the Middle East; although it's probably more likely it was brought back by a crusader.

5. Marc Morris, *A Great and Terrible King.*

6. Asbridge, *Knight.*

7. Asbridge, *Knight.*

8. Christopher Hibbert, *The English: A Social History.*

9. Poole, *From Domesday.*

10. Poole, *From Domesday.*

11. Asbridge, *Knight.*

12. Poole, *From Domesday.*

13. William Marshal, *L'Histoire de Guillaume le Marechal.*

Chapter 6

1. John Gillingham, *Conquest, Catastrophe and Recovery.*

2. I say that there is a fair bit of evidence that even in the twelfth and thirteenth centuries, England was moving away from a peasant society, outlined in Alan MacFarlane's *The Origins of English Individualism.*

3. Seward, *Brood.*

4. Marc Morris, *King John.*

5. At least it is considered unlikely.

6. Bridges, *Crusades.*

7. Dan Jones, *Realm Divided.*

8. Bridges, *Crusades.*

Chapter 7

1. William of Newburgh
2. Derek Wilson, *The Plantagenets.*
3. Poole, *From Domesday.*
4. Geoffrey Hindley, *A Brief History of Magna Carta.*
5. Or possibly only two years' worth. Opinion is divided.
6. Poole, *From Domesday.*

Chapter 8

1. Hervey Bagod, as quoted in Vincent.
2. Hindley, *History.*
3. The latest, 2013 figure.
4. Steven Pinker, *The Better Angels of Our Nature.*
5. He was rather the prototype of the rich kid who makes some spurious claim to be Irish or Native American.
6. It should be noted that the actual cause is disputed.
7. Castor, *She-Wolves.*
8. Bridges, *Crusades.*

Chapter 9

1. Castor, *She-Wolves.*
2. Written in 1220, in a book called *Historie des Ducs de Mornamdie et des Rois d'Angleterre.*
3. The *Romance of Fulk FitzWaryn* told the story of how they were playing chess, 'when John picked up the chessboard and hit Fulk with it. Fulk hit back, kicking John in the chest so hard that his head crashed against the wall, and he passed out.'
4. John, at five foot six inches, was roughly average for the time, although far shorter than his dashing elder brother.
5. Jones, *Plantagenets.*
6. Again, and confusingly, this might be ironic.
7. This is according to the biography of William Marshal, which was admittedly likely commissioned by William Marshal's son

William, who turned against John and so may have wanted to justify this by playing up his bad points.

8. This may be attaching a modern interpretation that did not exist at the time. Certainly his wife was very young, pre-teenage, and he was well into his thirties when they began sexual relations.

9. Jones, *Realm Divided*.

10. Poole, *From Domesday*.

11. Jones, *The Plantagenets*.

12. Nicholas Vincent, Magna Carta: *A Very Short Introduction*.

13. Accompanied by the notorious mercenary Mercadier, she managed to bring back her granddaughter Blancha, although Mercadier was killed by another mercenary on the way back.

14. Stephen Church, *King John*.

15. Church, *John*.

16. Church, *John*.

17. Poole, *From Domesday*.

18. Tombs, *English*.

19. It wasn't only babies who hit the bottle in medieval Europe, http://www.timeshighereducation.co.uk/features/it-wasnt-only-babies-who-hit-the-bottle-in-medieval-europe/177273.article.

20. Hibbert, *Social*.

21. Poole, *From Domesday*.

22. Poole, *From Domesday*.

Chapter 10

1. According to Roger of Wendover

2. Church, *John*.

3. Poole, *From Domesday*.

4. Harvey, *Plantagenets*.

5. James Hannam, *God's Philosophers*.

6. "Student Violence at the University of Oxford," Medievalists. net, http://www.medievalists.net/2013/05/09/student-violence-at-the-university-of-oxford/.

7. Innocent wrote to John in January the following year warning: 'Look, the bow is at full stretch. Beloved son, avoid the arrow which turns not back.'
8. Jones.
9. This could be a fanciful story according to some historians. Either way, he certainly killed him.
10. Stephen Church, *King John*
11. Hindley, *History*.
12. David Carpenter, *Magna Carta*.
13. Church, *John*.

Chapter 11
1. Poole, *From Domesday*.
2. Church, *John*.
3. Carpenter, *Magna Carta*.
4. Vincent, *Short*.
5. Poole, *From Domesday*.

Chapter 12
1. Jones, *Realm*.
2. http://www.british-history.ac.uk/london-record-soc/vol10/ix-xxxiv.
3. Carpenter, *Magna Carta*.
4. Seward, *Brood*.
5. Poole, *From Domesday*.
6. Gillingham, *Conquest, Catastrophe and Recovery*.
7. Morris, , King John.
8. This slacker image is rather undone by the evidence of his tireless (mis)rule.

Chapter 13
1. Gillingham, *Conquest, Catastrophe and Recovery*.
2. Daniel Hannan, *How We Invented Freedom*.

3. Gimson, Andrew, *Gimson's Kings and Queens*.
4. From *King John New Interpretations* by Nicholas Vincent.
5. Carpenter, *Magna Carta*.
6. "Global climates, the 1257 mega-eruption of Samalas Volcano, Indonesia, and the 1258 English food crisis," Royal Historical Society, http://royalhistsoc.org/calendar/global-climates-1257-mega-eruption-samalas-volcano-indonesia-1258-english-food-crisis/.
7. Gillingham, *Conquest, Catastrophe and Recovery*

Chapter 14

1. "The Magna Cara at 800," The Economist, http://www.economist.com/news/christmas-specials/21636510-how-did-failed-treaty-between-medieval-combatants-come-be-seen-foundation?fsrc=scn/tw/te/pe/ed/usesofhistory.
2. Carpenter, *Magna Carta*.
3. "The Meaning of Magna Carta since 1215, History Today," http://www.historytoday.com/ralph-v-turner/meaning-magna-carta-1215
4. Vincent, *Short*.
5. Edward Channing, *A History of the United States*.
6. Dan Hannan, "As American as the year 1215," *Washington Examiner*, November 17, 2014. http://www.washingtonexaminer.com/as-american-as-the-year-1215/article/2556151#.VGobUk_nrZY.twitter.

Chapter 15

1. "Magna Carta edition found in Sandwich archive scrapbook," BBC News. http://www.bbc.co.uk/news/uk-england-31242433.
2. Vincent, *Short*.